The Vegan Agenda Exposed

How Plant-Based Diets Contribute to Premature Aging, Physical Degeneration, & Serve "The Great Reset"

By Varis Ahmad

The Vegan Agenda Exposed

The content contained within this book may not be reproduced, duplicated or transmitted without direct written permission from the author or publisher.

Under no circumstances will any blame or legal responsibility be held against the publisher, or author, for any damages, reparation, or monetary loss due to the information contained within this book. Either directly or indirectly.

Legal Notice:
This book is copyright protected. This book is for personal use. This book, or parts thereof, may not be reproduced in any form without permission. Published in The United States.

Disclaimer Notice:
All information and material published in this book, *The Vegan Agenda Exposed How Plant-Based Diets Contribute to Premature Aging, Autoimmune, Physical Degeneration & Serve "The Great Reset",* are for general health and educational purposes only. The content and statements contained within this book have not been evaluated by The FDA and are only the authors opinions. You are encouraged to confirm the information contained herein with other sources. This information is not meant to be a substitute for medical advice. If you have underlying medical conditions please seek advise before implementing any of the protocols outlined in this book. The information is not intended to replace medical advise offered by physicians. If you choose to use the information available in this book with-out the prior consent of your physician, you are agreeing to accept the full responsibility for your decisions. The author will not be liable for any direct, indirect, special, exemplary, or other damages, arising therefrom.

Copyright © 2022 Varis Ahmad
All rights reserved.

The Vegan Agenda Exposed

CONTENTS

Introduction   7

Chapter 1: Plants Toxins & Biochemical Defense Mechanisms   17

Chapter 2: Grains, Bread, Depleted Soils, & a Toxic Staple   32

Chapter 3: Plant Defense Compounds, Autoimmune Diseases, & Leaky-Gut   44

Chapter 4: Fruit-Sugar, Premature Aging & Disease   52

Chapter 5: Animals Foods vs Plant Foods Nutrient Composition   67

Chapter 6: Analysis of Human, Carnivore & Herbivorous Digestive Systems   88

Chapter 7: Anthropological Records & Human Desire for Animal Fat   98

Chapter 8: Saturated Animal Fat & Cholesterol are The Most Anti-Aging, Brain-Building, & Health-Enhancing Nutrients Available to Humans   109

Chapter 9: Metabolism, Carbohydrates, Energy, & Obesity   119

Chapter 10: The Cholesterol, Saturated Fat, & Heart-Disease Myth   132

Chapter 11: Government & Corporate Collusion,   140

Dietary Propaganda, & Statins

Chapter 12: Toxic Vegetable-Oils Replacing 145
Nourishing Animal Fats

Chapter 13: Critiquing The China Study 160

Chapter 14: The Politicization of Veganism 163
& The Great Reset

Chapter 15: Dietary Solutions Amongst a 173
Sea of Nutritional Dogma

Chapter 16: Livestock Farming as an Environmental 177
Solution for a Dying Planet

Chapter 17: The Ethical Debate 187

Conclusion 189

The Vegan Agenda Exposed

INTRODUCTION

In recent years, plant-based, vegan and vegetarian diets, have garnered much publicity, attention and favor. They have received the patronage of governments, corporate media, multinational corporations and international health organizations. Vegan diets have also become very popular amongst youth who receive their information from youtube "celebrities" and popular Netflix films, which advocate for plant-based or vegan diets. Massive public relations campaigns associate such plant-based diets with health and longevity. This book is a challenge to the mythical narrative associating vegan diets with health and longevity. I propose instead, that vegan diets are amongst the most malnourishing and least healthful diets ever conceived of by man, even worse than the diets advocated by official government food pyramids.

It is true, that individuals who remove packaged and processed foods from their diet, will inevitably experience greater health on a whole-plant-foods. This should come as no surprise. Many vegans remove sodas, cookies, crackers, donuts, and chips, in favor of fruits and vegetables with claims of miraculous health benefits. This is very reasonable.

Health is not an off and on switch, but a vertical spectrum. There are varying degrees of health. A person becomes healthier or less healthy. Each degree is dependent on a persons diet, nourishment, lifestyle and age. As a person fortifies their nutritional reserves, they experience greater degrees of health, vitality, strength, intelligence, fertility and well-being. This process of attaining higher levels of health and well-being, we can term nourishment and physical development. Conversely, the process of experiencing lesser levels of health, well-being and vitality, we can term as aging and physical degeneration. Vegans diets do not offer higher levels of health and development. They in fact, subject individuals to premature aging and advanced physical degeneration for the many reasons that will be expanded upon in this book.

The plant-based and vegan diets which have become so popular today, offer only very limited ranges of health and development. They are great for a time if a person wishes to lose weight and detoxify, but they do not nourish and build. They do not fortify and regenerate the strength of the mind and body. They do not contribute to further development and fortification. In fact, they limit and even inhibit human development. Vegan diets are not sufficient enough to properly develop human beings and fulfill their genetic potential.

To fulfill our genetic potential, is to blossom and develop the fullness of our spiritual and physical being. All living organisms in wild nature, or objective reality, blossom and thrive by obeying natural law. As I will expose in this book, the vegan diet is entirely against natural law. The nutritional advise touted by so called "health experts" and government agencies are against natural law. Their dietary guidelines are the antithesis to a human appropriate diet. The United States Food Pyramid and the vegan diet are famine diets when contrasted to the nutritional requirements necessary for optimal human health and genetic fulfillment. In objective reality or wild nature, excessive plant foods were only consumed in times of famine when no animal foods were available.

    Novel ideas of plant-based or vegan diets sound revolutionary, but the fact of the matter is, that the general public has in fact subsisted off of such plant-based diets for the entirety of their lives. The food pyramid advocated by governments not only in the United States but much of the industrialized world has been, and is in fact, plant-based. The removal of meats and animal foods from the diet is not the dramatic and extreme transition it has been made out to be. The majority of industrialized peoples, especially Americans, are already on plant-based diets and have been so for the last 100 years. The foundation of the food pyramid has been plant foods. The transition to veganism is only the last step in a long line of transitions away from what constitutes a natural human diet. See the food pyramid below.

    Diets such as those advocated in official government food pyramids, by vegan and plant-based pundits, do not have much to do with health or science, as much as they have to do with vegan religious ideals, as well as, corporate profits and lobbyist. They in fact have no historical precedent. These diets which advocate for the copious consumption of indigestible plant foods and the removal of nutrient-dense animal foods, are unheard of and alien when we study the dietary anthropology of isolated and primitive tribes. Isolated and primitive tribes do not suffer from the same degenerative diseases as we do in the Modern West. The plant-based food pyramid and vegan diets, starve the population of nutrition. Nutrition which is critical for our health, mental and physical integrity, happiness, longevity and well-being.

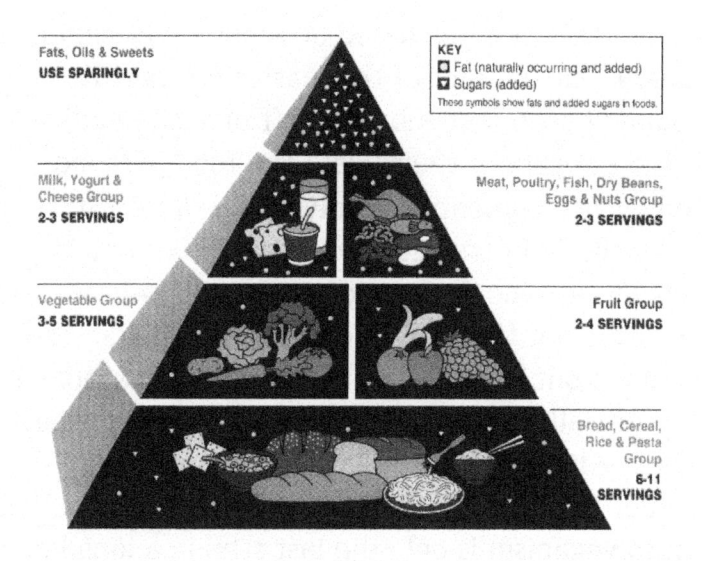

Fats, Oils & Sweets
USE SPARINGLY

KEY
☐ Fat (naturally occurring and added)
☑ Sugars (added)
These symbols show fats and added sugars in foods.

Milk, Yogurt & Cheese Group
2-3 SERVINGS

Meat, Poultry, Fish, Dry Beans, Eggs & Nuts Group
2-3 SERVINGS

Vegetable Group
3-5 SERVINGS

Fruit Group
2-4 SERVINGS

Bread, Cereal, Rice & Pasta Group
6-11 SERVINGS

The 1st world nations which have advocated for plant-based diets and the removal of animal fats, have seen skyrocketing statistics in regards to autoimmune disorders and degenerative diseases. These diseases and disorders correlate perfectly with the dietary trends over the course of the 20th century, which were characterized by the anti-cholesterol propaganda, the removal of animal foods, and their substitution with various forms of plant foods. The novel plant foods were introduced to the modern diet in the form of refined carbohydrates, indigestible vegetation, seed-oils, refined sugars, hybridized fruits, genetically modified grains amongst many others.

The reader should call to mind the contents inside all modern groceries and markets. There are a dozen or so aisles of packaged and processed foods, made entirely of plant foods such candies, crackers, pastas, chips and so on. A large section dedicated to fresh produce and vegetation, and finally a small refrigerated section in the corner of the market reserved for meats and dairies of different kinds.

A few of the epidemics which we now face in America as a result of the ill-founded plant-based food pyramid are:

- Autism diagnosis which was 1 in 5000 in 1975, is now 1 in 36, and expected to be 1 in 3 by 2035.

- Cancer rates have skyrocketed, doubling in only the last 15 years. Today 1 in 2 Americans are diagnosed with cancer and that number is set to climb to 4 in 5 by 2035. One of the largest killers of children today is cancer.

- In 1965, 4% of the population had chronic disease diagnosis, today 46% of children are diagnosed with chronic diseases.

- Attention Deficit is diagnosed in 1 in 8 children.

- Diabetes is diagnosed in 1 in 4. Type 2 diabetes used to be called adult onset diabetes because it was only diagnosed in adults, today 2 in 3 people contracting it are children and young people. It used to take 40 to 60 years in order for the bodies to degenerate due to sugar problems, today it is occurring in 5 in 10 years.

- Obesity plagues 1 in 3 people.

- Autoimmune disorders such as multiple sclerosis, irritable bowel syndrome, and celiac have boomed in recent decades.

- Infertility rates amongst men and women are sky rocketing. 1 in 4 women are infertile, 1 in 3 men are infertile. Male sperm concentration has dropped by more than half over the course of the 20th century and is continuing to plummet. As a species we are losing the ability to procreate and it has entirely to do with our diets, nutrition and environment. If we do not change, we will not survive.

We can not attribute to diet alone all of these disease endemics, but they have most definitely played a contributory role in the degeneration of the public's health. It is absurd to believe that the little amounts of meat already in the diet are the culprit for the modern degenerative disease endemics. As I explained earlier, these diseases coincide with the introduction of more plant foods into the diet over the coarse of the 20th century.

Government agencies, public health organizations, and so called "science and studies" performed at the prestigious universities of the developed world, have failed utterly in regards to care taking public health. They have insisted to the public that the little amounts of animal foods which have been present in the diets of North Americans, are the culprits for all our diseases. Hundreds of billions of dollars are donated every year to research facilities and organizations dedicated to autoimmune disorders, cancer and other degenerative disease but to no avail. This is by design.

A healthy, well nourished, strong population, does not contribute to the economic well-being of the corporate-oligarchy. The corporate-oligarchy profits at the expense of public health. If heart disease and cancer were "cured", it would cause The American Economy to collapse overnight. There is much money to be made off of a sick populace. In a capitalistic system where nearly all moral and ethical codes have corroded, financial profit is the sole aim of all human action.

The idea that vegans, plant-based pundits and government organizations peddle onto the public is that animal foods have been responsible for our degenerative diseases. They even postulate that a plant-based or vegan diet, is the "natural" diet for human beings and is most suitable for our physiology. Public and government organizations such as The American Heart Association, insist that saturated animal fats, animal proteins, and cholesterol are the culprits for the cardiovascular disease endemic we have been facing in The United States. Most recently, international organizations such as The World Health Organization, released a study which associated consumption of red meat with cancer. The story was quickly parroted by media, tabloids, celebrity influencers, Netflix documentaries and government health agencies.

Nothing should be accepted as fact, as knowledge and understanding, until it is challenged by someone competent enough to challenge it. This book is a challenge to the ill-founded, unscientific, nutritional and dietary guidelines, which have become so popular as of late. This book is meant to serve as a guide and aid for all those who seek truth in regards to nourishing themselves, extending longevity, enhancing health and embracing life to the fullest extent possible. This work is especially relevant to parents who are raising young children, as they are most susceptible to nutritional deprivation at young ages.

This book also stands as a rallying call to all those interested in the health and well-being of The North American People. At present time, there is a very well organized and well funded movement intending to tax or remove meat from the diets of the public all-together. The meat-tax would essentially relegate meat as a food for the rich and privileged. There are very many motives for the removal of meat from the diet. The most important of these motives is the fact that those lacking in animal nutrients are more docile, weak-minded and easier to control. They make for better "citizens" who will readily regurgitate whatever line of thinking is spoon-fed to them by the corporate-oligarchy. It is important that keen individuals hear both sides of the story, in order to make their own, independent judgment calls.

    Although I will use studies to reinforce my points in this work, I wish to emphasize on just how unimportant they are. It is because of these "studies", that the public's health has degenerated to this most atrocious state which we find ourselves in now. You will find one health expert after another touting "studies" which prove the benefits of this or that superfood, this or that diet. Today, you can find a "study" to prove anything. There are research labs across the country whom specialize in orchestrating and manipulating data in order to publish studies with preconceived conclusions. Large multinational corporations ranging from the pharmaceutical and medical industries, to the mega-food corporations, use these labs to publish studies in order to garner public sentiment and favor for their products. University research labs are beholden to the whims and orders of their multinational corporate donors. If they do not comply, they do not receive funding.

    In addition to the studies which I will cite in this work, I will primarily use logic, reason, and objective observation of the natural world, in order to draw conclusions. All animals of the same species eat the same diets in wild nature. Every wolf eats the same species appropriate diet as every other wolf, varying only in the types of prey or wild animals available. Bee's in China consume the same type of nourishment as do bees in America, varying only by the type of flowers. Likewise, there is a species appropriate diet for human beings as well. Logic and reason will be our guiding compass in deconstructing the mythical vegan narrative.

This book is akin to a Ph.D. dissertation. Different, far ranging topics must be covered in order to understand the full picture, the full magnitude, of the orchestrated nutritional crisis and famine we are facing today. I will cover plant biochemistry, the anthropology of plant foods and their hybridization, the human digestive system and foods which are most suitable, the damaging effects of plant foods on human physiology, the lost art and science of artisan plant food preparation, the anthropology of nutrition and isolated cultures, the nutritional comparison between plant and animal foods, the introduction of new and unnatural plant foods into the diet and their correlation with disease, the health giving properties of meats and other animal foods, the ecological argument against animal foods, and finally, the motives for such orchestrated, dietary and nutritional starvation of the public.

CHAPTER 1

Plants Toxins & Biochemical Defense Mechanisms

We very often hear of the health benefits of plant foods. Yes, in proper portions, when properly prepared, and in conjunction with animal foods, they can be a great addition to any diet. Plant foods and carbohydrates can offer us with great nutritive qualities. Carbohydrates can be used as fuel, fresh fruit or vegetable juices can offer hydration, and plant fibers can help to clean the bowels. What is not very often mentioned is the harmful consequences of over consuming plant foods, such as in vegan diets or even The Standard American Diet. Plant foods, no matter how nutritive or tasty they may be, also pose significant threat to human physiology.

In Nature, all species are equipped with intrinsic qualities which allow for self-defense and self-preservation. Humans are upright standing creatures with brains capable of a higher form of intellect than that found in the animal world. Human intelligence is different than the instinctual intelligence of the plant and animal worlds. Humans have the ability to think, ponder, reflect, reason and conceptualize.

Humans are unique in their ability to develop spears, arrows, swords and other sharp tools, used for hunting and defense. Animals do not have such an ability but are equipped with fangs, claws, camouflage, the ability to flee, and other such traits, in order to aid in their defense and predation.

In the case of plants, which do not have the type of mechanical and dynamic qualities available to higher forms of life, we find a host of **biochemical** agents that damage the nervous system of predators. These natural, plant biochemicals, damage the nervous system, inhibit digestion, damage the gut-lining, disrupt physiology, poison organs, and trigger systemic inflammation throughout the body of humans and other obligatory carnivores who eat them. Plants do not have the ability to ward off prey by physical means and thus, nature has equipped them with biochemical means. All things in nature strive to survive, thrive and reproduce. Nothing wants to perish.

Vegan and plant-based pundits have brainwashed many youth today, with ideas that vegetation is mankind's original food. They argue without any scientific basis that human physiology is most compatible with plant foods and not animal foods. Many unsuspecting youth truly believe they are on "the healthiest diet", when in fact, they are on the complete opposite. They are on a famine diet. One that inhibits development, growth and maturation. The arguments of plant-based pundits rely on sentiment for the most part and use the variety of colors found in plant foods to make an appeal for "natural foods". They do not take into account that these very plant foods contain within them, intrinsic plant pesticides that are designed to harm human physiology. Plants have natural molecules which kill human cells. Plants do not want to be devoured.

In The Modern West, we find that our youth are subject to many food allergies. The reasons for this will be elaborated later on in this book, but it is interesting to note, that meat foods never appear on allergy tests. This is because meat is the most digestible food and does not exasperate autoimmune disorders. In fact, it is the primary food and is obligatory for human well-being. Majority of the foods listed on the results of allergy tests are plant foods, which include leafy greens, starches, seeds, grains, beans and nuts of different varieties. Milk and eggs are also included in allergy tests, but that is due to the poor quality of commercial produced dairy. Part of the reason for the food allergies are an overconsumption of plant toxins which damage the gut, leak through the gut-lining and challenge the immune system. The copious amounts of plant toxins consumed in a diet, drive and exasperate inflammation in an already nutritionally deprived and degenerated populace. The following is a list of plant toxins and is by no means comprehensive.

Categories of Plant Toxins	Examples	Effects
Flavonoids	Kaempferol, Quercetin	Inhibits metabolic enzymes
Endocrine Disruptors	Lectins, Phytoestrogens	Damage endocrine receptors
Anti-Nutrients	Oxalic Acids, Phytic Acid	Decrease nutrient availability, inhibit nutrient absorption, form kidney stones, irritate the gut
Immune Disruptors	Lectins, Gliadin, Saponins	Cause leaky gut, damage intestinal lining, damage nervous system

Cyanide is a well known poison. It handicaps cellular respiration and has the potential to kill in large doses. It is found naturally in plant foods such as cherries, plums, almonds and over 2500 plant species. Cyanide is released from plant tissues when it receives damage through chewing or predation. Corn, cherry, apricot, apple seeds and cassava are common domesticated plants with cyanide. These cyanides are used by the plants to deter animals from feasting too heavily on them.

Phytic Acid is a natural substance found in all plant seeds. This includes all nuts, seeds, beans and grains, as they are all essentially seeds. Seeds are programmed by nature to survive and reproduce in order to perpetuate their species. Their survival mechanisms include a host of plant toxins, the most common and prevalent being phytic acid.

In seeds, phytic acid is bound to phosphorus. This means the phosphorus is unavailable. Phytic Acid is referred to as an anti-nutrient in nutritional science due to it's ability to bind to minerals and make them unavailable. Phosphorus is a crucial mineral needed for energy or ATP production, health of bones, proper development and growth of all bodily tissues, biosynthesis of all proteins and more. The highest quality source of phosphorous is animals foods, where as in plant foods, they are very scarce and even unavailable due to phytic acid's binding properties.

To make matters even worse, phytic acid binds to minerals from other foods in the digestive tract such as calcium, iron and zinc. It is in essence a mineral binder and makes them unavailable to the human digestive tract. The bed rock of The Standard American and vegan diets rely on grains and beans, creating very mineral deplete and malnourished people.

Oxalic Acid is a poisonous crystalline organic compound, found in the highest concentrations in leafy greens, and to a lesser extent in fruits, nuts, seeds and beans. They are exclusive to plant foods. Oxalic Acid is referred to in nutritional science as an anti-nutrient due to its nutrient binding effects. When consumed in large quantities, these oxalates bind to calcium and iron in the digestive tract, forming calcium oxalate and iron oxalate.

These are small crystalized stones that the body can not incorporate into its physiology and must be excreted. In ideally healthy individuals who are consuming plant foods in moderation, oxalates are excreted through stool and urine. In plant-based and vegan eaters, oxalates accumulate and form kidneys stones, and also lead to systemic calcification of organs, glands and arteries. The process of juicing large amounts of green vegetables makes people especially susceptible to oxalate poisoning as it concentrates large amounts of these oxalates in the juices.

Lectins are one of the most powerful plant defense mechanisms. They are proteins bound to the carbohydrates found exclusively in plant foods, but are highest in grains and beans. They are also referred to as anti-nutrients in nutritional science. Their first mode of action is binding to cells in the intestinal lining and destroying them. Even after cooking, they cause issues which is why bloating, gas and indigestion, are so common after consuming beans. Although the initial consequence of consuming lectins is leaky gut, persistent consumption leads to systemic organ damage. There are many studies which show lectins binding to and damaging reproductive organs of infertile females.[1]

Lectins are resistant to stomach acid and do not break down. Soaking and cooking beans reduces some levels of lectins but never all. Some beans such as kidney beans have the potential to cause severe adverse reactions. Studies have shown that a diet of only 1% raw kidney beans will kill a rat in two weeks. When individuals experience flatulence and bloating after consuming beans, it is a symptom of intestinal damage due to lectins in the beans.

---

[1] Klentzeris LD; Bulmer JN; Li TC; Morrison L; Warren A; Lectin Binding of Endometrium in Women with Unexplained Infertility.PMID: 1915939, 1991. https://pubmed.ncbi.nlm.nih.gov/1915939/.

Further, lectin binds to minerals in the digestive tract, making them unavailable for absorption. It has also been demonstrated by researchers for decades now, that lectins can leak through the gut, transport through the vagus nerve and damage the brain. Such forms of brain damage ultimately contribute to reduced mental function, mental illness's and degenerative diseases such as Parkinson's and Alzheimers.[2]

We must remember when learning of these toxic plant chemicals that this is what nature intended for them to do. The intended use of these plant toxins was to help plants ward off predators, who are unfit for consumption of these plant foods. The fact that they have been demonstrated to damage all organs of the body should come as no surprise but as a sobering, logical understanding of natures realities. The question instead should be why is their a public relations campaign insisting that we consume these non-foods as the bedrock of our diet? Why have these anti-nutrients been rebranded to the public as phytonutrients (plant nutrients)?

PhytoEstrogens are plant compounds which mimic female hormones and are also a form of plant defense. They are a type of fungicide which is designed to kill or ward off predation. Plants have been shown to release more when they are under attack.

Soy, which is a staple in vegan diets, is a plant that is highly concentrated in phytoestrogens. In traditional oriental cultures, soy was fermented and used only as a condiment

---

[2] Zheng, Jolene, et al. Dietary Plant Lectins Appear to Be Transported from the Gut to Gain Access to and Alter Dopaminergic Neurons of Caenorhabditis Elegans, a Potential Etiology of Parkinson's Disease. *Frontiers*, Frontiers, 1 Jan. 1AD, https://www.frontiersin.org/articles/10.3389/fnut.2016.00007/full.

and flavor enhancer, never as a food. It is notorious for causing hormonal and endocrine disruption. Some of the symptoms include reproductive problems, the development of masculine traits in women and feminine traits in men, sperm reduction and polycystic ovary syndrome (PCOS).[3]

Although it may seem odd, soy and many other plants high in phytoestrogen cause people to be more susceptible to brainwashing, emotional appeal and sensationalism. It causes people to lose the ability to discern logically and intelligently. This is due to the estrogenic effects on the brain from a diet high in phytoestrogens. Nearly all vegan "meats" are pseudo-meats made of soy. Individuals subject to high phytoestrogens can become more emotional, less rational, quick to anger and extremely sensitive.

"Soya isoflavones are clearly endocrine disrupting, but although they are similar to their
synthetic brethren in terms of their cellular and molecular mechanisms of action on neuroendocrine structure and function, and the scope of adverse outcomes they can inflict, society embraces these compounds at the same time it rejects, often with vigour, exposure to their synthetic brethren."- *Heather B. Patisaul, Department of Biological Sciences, Center for Human Health and the Environment, NC State University, Raleigh, NC 27695, USA*

Cruciferous Vegetables and Sulforaphane are a family of plants that belong to the Brassicaceae family which include kale, broccoli, cauliflower, bok choy, brussel sprouts, cabbage and other similar green vegetables. When these plants are cut or chewed, they release a compound called isothiocyanate (sulforaphane), which is a molecule

---

[3] "Endocrine Disruption by Dietary Phyto-oestrogens: Impact on Dimorphic Sexual Systems and Behavior." Heather B. Patisaul, Department of Biological Sciences, Center for Human Health and the Environment, NC State University, Raleigh, NC 27695, USA

designed to kill small living creatures. This molecule has of recent become the darling nutrient of the plant-based and vegan world. They do not realize that by consuming high quantities of such foods they are essentially on a pesticide diet that is killing their cells with every morsel of food.

When studied under a microscope, sulphoraphane is found to kill mutagens, microbes and other forms of microbial life. For this reason it is touted as a nutrient. Plant-based health authorities do not mention that this compound also kills healthy cells. It is essentially a form of plant chemotherapy. **It would be wise to include it in the diets off developed individuals who have forms of pathogenic disease but not in the diets of those who are in need of foods which contribute to growth and development. To develop properly, we need food which contributes to building new, healthy, and strong cells. Not foods which kill our cells.**

This compound poisons mitochondria and leads to chronic fatigue. Mitochondria are the power house and energy generators of our cells. The side effects of sulforaphane include:

- Poisoned Mitochondria
- Inhibition of Microsomal Enzymes
- Generate ROS
- Interfere with Iodine Thyroid Absorption
- Disrupt Epithelial Barriers (gut lining)
- Depletes Glutathione Levels
- Kills Healthy Cells

Protease Inhibitors are common constituents of all seeds, including grains, beans and legumes. Seeds develop protease inhibitors in order to disrupt and block enzymatic function of prey, wether they be insects, animals or humans. They affect digestion by inhibiting the activity of trypsin, protease and chymotrypsin in the human gastrointestinal system. These are primary enzymes secreted by the human stomach responsible for the digestion of proteins and fats of animal foods. The consumption of plant foods such as grains, beans, seeds and legumes which are rich in protease inhibitors, inhibit our ability to properly digest our proteins. **Protease inhibitors found in grains, beans and seeds paralyze the stomach.**

This compound also causes inflammation to the gut, indigestion of food and protein deficiency. Plant-based complete protein is a myth due to the low level of amino acids and the poor bioavailability of plant amino acids. Plant amino acids are made unavailable to human physiology due to the inhibitors and pesticides inherent to the plants. The plants do not want to be devoured. Animal flesh contains no sort of inhibitors, lectins or any of the aforementioned anti-nutrients. Animal foods are the most bioavailable foods available to man. I will elaborate more on human physiology and digestive process's later.

Nightshades are vegetables that contain a type of pesticide called **cholinesterase inhibitors**. These inhibitors very strongly bind to cholesterol and burst open cell membranes. They kill human cells by attacking the cell wall. Vegetables in the nightshade family include tomatoes, potatoes, eggplants, pepper and much more.

This is not to say that these foods should not be consumed at all. **Rather, they should be consumed in moderation next to animal foods which can buffer their negative side effects**. Issues arise from these foods when they are consumed in the context of vegan or plant-based diets. It is very common to find people, especially vegans, who develop allergies to nightshade vegetables. The removal of meat inevitably forces individuals to substitute the missing calories with more toxic plants. **Nightshade**

vegetables such as tomatoes, peppers and eggplants burst and destroy human cells in the brain, skin, gut and other various organs.

Starches are plant foods such as potatoes, grains, breads, tubers and roots. Historically they have played an important role in many healthy human cuisines and diets. Many proponents of veganism advocate for people to sustain themselves on starch-based diets while removing all animal fats. The Standard American diet is also a starch-based diet reliant on grains, cereals, breads, in addition to low-fat dietary guidelines. These people take no consideration of the fact that all human cultures who incorporated starches into their diet, did so in addition to their fatty animal foods. They also went to great lengths to properly prepare starch foods. Without proper preparation and the addition of animal fat, starchy foods cause incredible damage to the intestinal lining.

Healthy cultures consumed bread using properly prepared grains such as wheat, barely and rye. These grains were soaked, sprouted, ground to a flour and fermented, resulting in popular artisan breads such as sourdough. This process disables some of the anti-nutrients found in these grains. When grains are soaked and sprouted, they begin to disable some of their defense compounds, although they are still not digestible at that point. The additional step of grinding grains to a flour and then fermenting them with yeast, further disables their defense compounds.

When yeast is added to flour, it begins to break down. Yeast predigest the flour for us, making it more digestible. This is what sourdough bread is. **Sourdough bread is plant seeds which has been predigested for us by yeast, because we can not digest these foods ourselves.** We eat the excrement of the yeast. Compare this to the modern diet and bread, where the grains are commercially produced and prepared without taking these traditional preparation methods. This undigestible food is the basis of The American Food Pyramid. The breads are not properly prepared, nor are they grown using proper methods.

In addition to this very important preparation process, traditional cultures consumed breads in conjunction with very large amounts of animal fats in order to buffer the abrasive nature of starch particles on the digestive tract. Sourdough and butter, or bread and cream cheese, are very common traditional dishes I am alluding to here.

Starches such as potatoes are in the night shade family of plants and contain plant pesticides such as lectins, nitrates and glycoalkaloids. These plant pesticides are incredibly damaging to the gut, cause gas, bloating and general digestive discomfort. Potatoes too were normally cooked and consumed in butter in order to enhance their digestibility and to buffer the irritating nature of toxic plant compounds. Today, the consumption of these foods have aggravated autoimmune diseases, due to public health agencies advising the public to reduce saturated animal fats in their diets. **The public has for decades been starved of those foods which are the least irritating and most nourishing, in lieu of those foods which are least nourishing and most irritating.** As I will explain later, this was done in order to secure corporate profits on a sick, mentally ill populace.

Meat Digestibility

In contrast to the myriad of plant defense chemicals which are designed to ward off predation, meats have no such anti-nutrient, or chemical defense constituent. Once an animal is hunted and neutralized there are no more defense mechanisms. Animals use their claws, teeth, and ability to run to defend themselves. The human being is not a grazing animal with his head in the grass twelve hours a day. The human being is an upright walking creature designed to hunt for several hours and enjoy most of his time as leisure. The human being is natures apex predator. Our ability to hunt nutrient-dense animal foods and not spend time grazing all day, is what contributed to our ability to develop amazing civilizations and works of art in our history. Our ability to design weapons, spears, arrows and traps is what allowed us to dominate the animal kingdom. We are designed by nature to do so.

Meat is digested with extreme ease even without cooking. Meat is the only food which creates no digestive discomfort when consumed either raw or cooked. Bloating, gas, and other discomfort in the gut are indicative of what is suitable for our physiology. A meal consisting of only meat will never cause gas or bloating. There are absolutely no anti-nutrients which would inhibit our digestion of meat or harm our physiology in any way. Furthermore, the human stomach and digestive tract are designed exactly for the digestion of meat. I will elaborate on this in a later chapter.

Raw meat dishes including raw beef, raw fish, raw pork and more, exist in traditional cultures all over the world. Conversely there are hardly any raw, plant-based dishes. Raw plant foods such as The Asian Mung Bean Sprout or The Middle Eastern Tabbouleh, are used merely as garnishes in supplementation to the main meat meals. They serve as flavor enhancers, additional water and exotic flavor. They are never the main meal.

However, raw meat dishes which serve as the main course are found all over the world. Such dishes include steak tartare (France), Yookhwe (Korea), Oseenworst (Netherlands), Koi Soi (Thailand), Bo Tai Chanh (Vietnam), Kitfo (Ethiopia), Kibbey Nayyeh (Lebanon/Middle East), Carne Apache (Mexico), Beef Carpaccio (Italy), Basashi (Japan) amongst countless others.

I will be mentioning traditional cultures, their cuisines, and dietary practices, throughout this book, because modern generations do not have any idea of what a traditional human diet looks like. Raised in the post-modern world, they do not have any connections with the past, with human culture and tradition. It is easy to fool such people with pictures of colorful fruits and vegetables, and claim that returning to a vegan lifestyle is a return to a more healthy pastime. The fact of the matter is, that the healthy and harmonious past time of our preindustrial ancestry was one where cultures emphasized the need to acquire nutrient-dense animal foods. Our ancestry understood that without these foods, we would simply fail to thrive and properly develop.

Aside from the consumption of very little, easy to digest raw plant foods, such as The Middle Eastern Salad and Oriental mung-bean sprout, the consumption of raw grains, beans, nuts, seeds and starches is nearly non-existent in traditional cultures and for good reason. These foods are poisonous and toxic to human physiology. When they are consumed they are properly prepared, fermented, and cooked well, in order to make these plant foods more digestible. **Even after going through proper preparation, they present a challenge to human physiology and were generally consumed in conjunction with animal fat in order to further buffer their harmful effects.**

I have only covered a few of the plant defense toxins in detail here. A more comprehensive analysis of the facts would require volumes of literature. My hope is that readers can grasp the idea that plant-based diets are not the "clean," "pure" and "healthy" cuisine that is advocated by modern currents of nutritional and dietary thought. Vegan diets are saturated with plant pesticides and toxins which are harmful to human biology, cause degenerative disease, and premature aging.

This is not to say I recommend eating no plants at all, although that may at times be necessary for those who are severely immune compromised with autoimmune disorders. Recent fad diets such as the carnivore diet, which excludes all plant foods, have become very popular as of late. The carnivore diet helps individuals due to the removal of plant toxins in the diet that would otherwise further exasperate autoimmune symptoms. The popularity of this diet has turnt vegan dogma onto its head and the internet is filled with the anecdotal evidence of thousands of individuals, who regained health after following a meat only style of eating.

It is my belief that plants should be a part of diet as medicine, garnish, flavoring and as a carbohydrate supplement to fill muscle glycogen. Plants are part of the cuisines of many cultures that are purported to have longevity and graceful aging. Although they are never the core of the diet or plant-based, they play a role as supplemental food and garnishment. No culture in the world was as out of touch with nature such as the modern one. None tried to live off of plant-based diets.

There are cultures such as The Inuit and Massai who subsisted off of animal foods only, but there are no cultures who subsisted off of plant foods only. There are cultures who lived in equatorial regions of the world who incorporated far more plant mass and carbohydrates in their diet than did other cultures, but again, it was in additional to very healthy animal foods.

The need for plant foods in the diet vary by individuals and their ancestral or constitutional make up. Individuals facing health challenges and autoimmune disorders would do well embarking on an elimination diet of plant foods for some time. Each person will have varying levels of tolerance to plant toxins. Reintroducing plants which are ancestrally consistent with individuals, would be the the most intelligent method of reincorporating carbohydrate or plant foods back into the diet, without inflammatory or autoimmune regression.

CHAPTER 2

Grains, Bread, Depleted Soils, & a Toxic Staple

Bread in it's modern commercial form, is perhaps the single biggest contributor to the modern autoimmune disease endemic. Grains and bread make the very foundation of the food pyramid and play the largest dietary factor in the North American Diet. Grains such as wheat have spawned entire generations of celiac, hyper-allergic, and immune compromised people. I will make a case in this chapter that everyone is allergic to modern wheat and would do better without it. Unfortunately, many individuals remove meat foods, believing they are the cause of their ill-health and symptoms. Usually, vegans have their health deteriorate as they are forced to rely even more so on breads, toxic plants, grains and sugars when removing animal foods.

Wheat was initially a survival food in the hunter-gatherer diet. It played a very small role and was hardly consumed. It is laborious to manually pick and harvest seeds which are indigestible and offer little to no nutritional value. This all changed with the advent of agricultural civilization. Wheat was grown in large fields and sustained entire civilizations. When consumed in traditional cultures of humanity's classical civilizations, it was grown in rich soil, and prepared with the utmost respect. This included a fermentation process through which yeast neutralized much of the anti-nutrients or plant toxins inherent in wheat.

To ferment, is to cause something to decay or breakdown by the action of micro-organisms. In the case of bread, yeast and bacteria was used to break down and predigest the wheat. It resulted in what we call today sourdough bread. Bread making became an art and a cultural tradition in order to make healthy, digestible food.

Furthermore, wheat was used primarily as a means of supplementing a diet that was high in animal fat. Traditional cultures understood the necessity of animal fats in the diet. They used properly prepared bread as vehicles to consume large amounts of fat-soluble vitamins. A great example of this are the isolated people of The Loetschental Valley in The Swiss Alps who would smear high amounts of high-vitamin butter on sourdough bread. These people were recorded by traveler, anthropologist and legendary nutritionist, Dr. Weston A. Price D.D.S. to be free of many of the degenerative diseases known to modern man. This practice of properly prepared bread consumed with dairy fat was practiced in very many parts of the world. It was practiced by The Central Asian nomadic Indo-Iranians, The nomadic Turks and Mongols, and is still practiced today amongst countless settled and nomadic cultures across Eurasia.

The use of animal fat in conjunction with bread, made their starchy, indigestible fibers, more soft and digestible, so that it did not cause tears in the intestinal lining. Today, wheat products are ground into a flour and baked into breads at commercial and industrial scale, without taking proper precautions. They do not ferment them properly. The fermentation process is an artisan skill. Nearly all breads in super markets today are incredibly indigestible foods which develop and exasperate autoimmune diseases.

Furthermore, because the public has been manipulated into fearing animal fat, the consumption of breads without the aid or buffer of these animal fats causes even more harm. A grain based, or bread based diet, devoid of animal fat such as the one advocated by The USDA Food Pyramid or vegan "health authorities", would have been considered a famine diet in normal, healthy cultures, who were in tune with their bodies and the natural world.

The Advent of Modern Frankenstein Wheat and Petrochemical Agricultural Practices

To understand why modern wheat has such degenerative effects on the human body, we have to understand soil biology and modern agricultural practices. In preindustrial cultures that had a connection to soil and land, it was understood that the health of the soil was directly correlated with the health of the people. Animal manure and rock dust were used to add biological life and minerals to soil reserves. Healthy soil is very rich in microbial life and minerals. A single handful of soil from a healthy forest has up to 50 billion microorganisms.

Plants consume nutrients and minerals in the soil through their roots using micro-organisms. Micro-organisms are the metabolic machinery and digestive organs of the soil, the forest floor and plant roots. In a forest, an animal dies on the forest floor and microbial life decompose the body, feeding the soil and plants. When animals pass their feces onto the forest floor, mico-organisms break down the feces and feed the soil and plants. When organic matter such as the leaves of the forest fall to the floor, again, micro-organisms decompose this organic matter and feed soil and plant roots. The soil, the plants, and the microbes, are eating the animals, their manure, and all organic matter which falls to the forest floor. There is a cycle of life that is working seamlessly in nature, with or without mans existence. It a self sustaining, perfect, looped system.

The health of soil, plants, animals and humans, start with the microbiology of the soil. Minerals are essentially rocks in the soil. Plants, animals and humans do not have the metabolic or digestive machinery to break down minerals from rocks. In Nature, this is one of the roles relegated to micro-organisms. In healthy soil, there is a symbiosis between plant roots and the micro-organisms.

Micro-organisms break down minerals into simple compounds in the soil and deliver them to plant roots. In exchange, plant roots feed these micro-organisms with simple sugars. As a plant grows and develops, it embodies these minerals into it's structure. From the plant, these minerals are passed on and assimilated into the bodies of herbivorous animals and ruminants who have the digestive ability to break apart these plants using intestinal flora.

Human beings do not have the ability to break apart and absorb plants or minerals in the form of hard rocks. We do not have the metabolic machinery and digestive system required to break them down. **We do not have the metabolic ability to neutralize the plant toxins, digestive inhibitors and anti-nutrients present in plant foods. Nature has relegated the job of digesting plant material to herbivorous creatures who graze twelve hours a day, and convert plant material or carbohydrates, into protein and fat.** I will go into more detail about the digestive systems of herbivores, carnivores and humans in a later chapter.

The issue with modern agricultural practices began in the 1930's with The Dust Bowl Chronicles, which severely damaged the American and Canadian prairies and plains. Due to improper and unsustainable farming techniques, soil biology and mineral reserves were eroded over generations leaving the plains barren, devoid of life and humus. **Every time crops are harvested from a field, we take with the harvest a portion of the life giving properties, minerals, soil microbes, and organic matter from the field.**

Our crops had been grown and harvested on an industrial scale, which had led to rapid nutrient and top-soil depletion of North America's agricultural lands. Without resupply or refortification, these farms became barren, moister-less, nutrient-devoid soil, which was quick to turn to dust when high winds approached. This caused massive dust storms in our Nations farm fields, which later came to be known as The Dust Bowl Chronicles. It became nearly impossible to grow grains in these soils. In order to continue to grow grains and crops in our soil, we would have needed to treat the land holistically using regenerative agricultural techniques.

During the years of the Dust Bowls, brilliant researchers and scientist such as Dr. Weston A. Price, had conducted studies on the nations soils and crops, and reported that North American agricultural lands had on average thirty times less nutrients than those foods grown in isolated regions of the world. It has now been nearly one-hundred years that scientist have been raising alarm bells over nutrient depleted soils and foods. Dr. Weston A. Price had warned that The Western Nations were in danger of grave nutritional malnourishment. One-hundred years later, I can confidently state that the dangers now are far more dire than ever, and that we are at the brink of a precipitant. Landmark books such as *Empty Harvest* by Dr. Bernard Jenson MD, document the degenerative process's our soils have been subject to.

The solution to North America's soil degradation was addressed by The State and Mega-Food producers through the development of superphosphate fertilizers, pesticides, and herbicides. The Dust Bowl marked the beginning of chemical agriculture. The advent of superphosphate fertilizers allowed farmers to grow more food which appeared robust. It seemed like a wonderful innovation at the time, but we are dealing with the consequences today.

Superphosphate fertilizers or NPK, fortify a plant with large doses of three nutrients: nitrogen, phosphorus and potassium. The three of these nutrients combined in high doses give farmers the ability to grow large, robust plants, that are totally devoid of nutrition. Plants need a wide spectrum of nutrients and minerals from the soil to not only develop size, but also robust health. In healthy soil, wheat is able to accumulate around 96 minerals from the soil. Modern wheat is fertilized using just three nutrients which allow farmers to grow crops in dead soil. These crops give the appearance of large, healthy vegetables, but are in fact totally devoid of nutrition. The use of these fertilizers without trace mineral and biological replenishment further aggravated nutrient depletion of soils. Every time crops are grown and harvested from a field, there is further depletion of soil nutrients.

With passing years these large, robust, super phosphate fertilized crops, began to become more susceptible to disease. Modern crops are akin to bodybuilders who use steroids to develop large bodies, but lack totally in the underlying nutrition needed to support and sustain such size. It is unnaturally attained and not sustainable. The building blocks needed to support such large system are lacking. Disease, premature aging and systemic organ failure are very common in athletes that abuse steroids and we can draw a parallel with modern agriculture.

North America's agricultural fields also began to sprout forth dormant weeds in large quantities. In Nature, the land and soil bring forth weeds in order to try to heal and repair itself. This was a problem for the farmers, as it took up room which would otherwise be used for crop cultivation. The bottom line in modern chemical agriculture, is not healthy food or soil, but money and yield. To address the issue of disease and wild weeds, agricultural scientist introduced glyphosate to farmers. Glyphosate is sprayed on wheat and many other crops that are susceptible to disease. Glyphosate kills plant and bacterial life. In turn, we not only have depleted soils, but dead soils, with no microbial life. It is microbial life that drives the nutrition cycle in the soil. The plants gown in our fields are reliant entirely on chemical agriculture. The soils are dead.

At the time of their emergence, all of the chemical farming innovations were heralded as "The Green Revolution". Modern wheat has been modified to be able to withstand herbicides and pesticides. The constitution of human physiology consists of ten bacterial cells to one human cell. It is erroneous to believe that the glyphosate sprayed on our food to kill weeds and bacteria, has no effect on our own biology. In fact, there is ample research showing that indeed glyphosate is deleterious to human health. Glyphosate inhibits enzymatic activity of bacterial and plant life, which are necessary for growth. We are a macrocosm of bacterial life. Ingesting glyphosate from non-organic foods, causes inhibited development and mutagenic effects within our own bodies. **In summary, wheat is grown with life-support petro-chemicals, in dead, infertile soil, with no nutrients, and with large doses of herbicides which are antagonistic to biological life. Wheat has become the basis of the food pyramid and a staple of most plant-based and vegan diets.**

Gluten

The last and perhaps the most concerning perversion of wheat is in its hybridization. Different strains of wheat from distant countries were crossed and hybridized to form a new variation of wheat. This new variation was shorter, produced more wheat, and had a substantially higher yield. An unintended consequence of this was the increase of the gluten content in modern wheat, that is on average nine to fifteen times higher than heirloom wheat.

The problem with gluten is that it is absolutely indigestible by the human gut. When passing through the human digestive tract, undigested gluten rips and tears microvilli responsible for absorption of nutrients, as well as, the destruction of epithelial cells responsible for integrity of the gut lining. There has been ample work done on this subject and books published such as *Grain Brain* by Dr. David Perlmutter MD and *Wheat Belly* by Dr. William Davis MD.

Gluten is a protein found in wheat that is not subject to human digestive enzymes. It passes through the digestive tract undigested. It is a glue-like material which binds the starch and proteins in wheat. Dr. Rodeny Ford, MB., BS., MD., FRACP, is a pioneer in the field of pediatric food allergies and is of the assertion that no human body can digest gluten. He has given a phenomenal Tedx lecture available on youtube titled *Daily Bread- Can Any Human Body Handle Gluten?* Dr. Rodeny Ford asserts that this gluten triggers autoimmune diseases.

His scientific assertions are based on decades of research with children and adults. He found that stunted growth and bloated belly, are the most common and initial symptoms in children developing celiac disease. He has done research on thousands of children who came through his clinic and were put on a gluten-free diet. These were children who were not diagnosed with celiac. 80% got better on a gluten free diet. He concluded that majority of the symptoms associated with gluten consumption were due to nerve damage. The consumption of modern, frankenstein wheat, is essentially damaging the intestinal lining, all organs, and nervous system of the body.

Dr. Alessio Fasano is a world-renowned pediatric gastroenterologist and researcher. He currently holds many roles including but not limited to, Professor of Pediatrics at Harvard Medical School and serves as the director of the

Center for Celiac Research and Treatment at MassGeneral Hospital for Children. His work and research shows that **everybody** who eats gluten gets an inflammatory reaction in their gut by measuring the production of zonulin. Zonulin is a chemical excreted by the gut when cell walls are torn apart, causing leaky gut. Gluten is essentially tearing apart the gut.

In the 1960's, the tools needed for small bowel biopsy were developed. This is where a tube is inserted into the intestines, extracting a piece of tissue for examination and study under a microscope. What scientist discovered was that the tissue or villi (small microscopic finger like projections used for absorbing nutrients) were destroyed. The condition was termed villis atrophy. Celiac disease was coined but was compartmentalized into gastroenterology. Instead of addressing the cause of villis atrophy due to environmental and dietary causes, it was relegated to being a disorder and disease of the gut, for which we have no solution or cure. From there, it was then capitalized on by the medical establishment and their never ending supply of pharmaceuticals which do not prevent or reverse any disease.

Individuals are not diagnosed by the medical establishment with celiac disease until the entire intestinal lining and microvilli are destroyed. If a portion or only 90% of the villi are destroyed, it does not warrant a celiac diagnoses. This is teetering on the verge of insanity. The loss and damage of micro villi impedes our ability to properly absorb nutrients and leads to multiple nutrient deficiencies. This process takes years to develop and likewise, years to recover from. It causes stunted development and mentation. The very fabric of the intestinal lining and integrity of the body are coming apart with every morsel of bread consumed.

Because gluten can not be digested, it enters the small intestine where it wreaks havoc along the intestinal wall. The destruction of these villi and integrity of intestinal lining contribute to the development of every autoimmune disorder and gastrointestinal disease. There are different names for gastrointestinal diseases such as celiac, ulcerative colitis, crohns disease, irritable bowel syndrome, and so on. All can be characterized as a relative level of intestinal compromise and damage. All are various levels of disease advancement into the gut by way of environmental toxins, plant toxins and nutritional deprivation.

Although gluten is the most damaging of plant compounds, all the plant toxins mentioned in the previous chapter contribute to, or exasperate intestinal damage to one degree or another. Healthy cultures could consume proper portions of properly prepared grains and beans in their diets, because they did not experience the same type of intestinal disintegration modern people are subject to. They consumed adequate amounts of animal fats which are foundational to constantly renewing the cells in the intestines. They also took the utmost care in preparing plant foods through fermentation process's so that they did not pose harm. They were built differently and consumed proper foods.

An unpublished experiment carried out in 1960 by the researchers at The University of Michigan, found very disturbing results with rats that were fed cereals. Cereals are grain-based foods made of wheat or corn most often. The study was presented to a Senate Committee in 1972. In the study the laboratory was given 18 rats to experiment with and were divided into three groups. One group of rats received water and cornflakes, another group received water and the box that the cornflakes came in, and the final group was given water and rat chow.

The rats who were given rat chow sustained good health through out the experiment. The rats eating the cardboard cereal box became fatigued, lethargic, and eventually died of starvation. **The rats that were eating water and cornflakes cereals all died before the rats that were consuming the cardboard cereal box.** The rats eating the cereal developed abnormal behavior, bit each other, and attempted to gnaw on each other's brains, experienced convulsions, and finally premature death! Autopsy of the rats revealed pancreas, kidney and liver dysfunction, as well as degeneration of the spine and nerves.[4]

The conclusion of the study was that there was more nutrition in the cardboard box than in the cereal. I would argue, that the conclusion should have been that the cereal is more poisonous than consuming cardboard boxes. This is the healthy plant-based "food" which America's children consume on a daily basis. These foods are the bedrock for vegans and vegetarian diets. Over the course of the 20th century, The American Breakfast had steak and eggs replaced with commercially produced toxic-grains and cereals. This transition had nothing to do with science and health but rather it had to do with the mega-food producers and their corporate lobbying for the FDA.

To conclude on gluten, I must reiterate here that by now multiple generations of Americans have subsisted off of a toxic staple. The USDA food pyramid for over 50 years now has recommended a low-fat diet, with 6 to 11 serving of wheat and other grains daily. This is nothing short of nutritional deprivation. It has been official government policy to force this toxic staple into people's homes, and it is not at all backed by science or data, but instead by commercial

---

[4] Choate, Robert B. "Too Stuffed for Supper". Testimony Before the Senate Commerce Committee, Subcommittee on the Consumer. Council on Children, Media, and Merchandising, Washington, D.C. 2 Mar 72 69. P
https://files.eric.ed.gov/fulltext/ED059631.pdf

interests. Naturally, vegans who exclude animal products are forced to consume even greater amounts of this toxic staple. For readers who want to further their understanding of wheat's association with degenerative disease, I highly recommend a recent groundbreaking documentary titled, *Whats with Wheat*. It covers far more than what I could in a single chapter. It is available online and includes leading thinkers, researchers, physicians and scientist on this subject from around the world.

CHAPTER 3

Plant Defense Compounds, Autoimmune Diseases, & Leaky Gut

I am of the opinion that nearly every person in the country has some form of intestinal damage that could be diagnosed by the medical profession. One of the initial symptoms of leaky gut is acne and boils forming on the face. Other benign symptoms are dandruff, which is indicative of fungal infections (candida) taking hold in a compromised gut. These symptoms have been relegated to dermatology, but they are in fact associated with the gut and are autoimmune related. Unfortunately, the medical establishment can not offer any solutions for any gastrointestinal disorder. This is readily acknowledged by them, yet they will without question prescribe a cocktail of pharmaceuticals.

Aside from dietary induced intestinal degradation, intestinal degradation also occurs when beneficial gut flora are killed off by environmental toxins, petroleum based pesticides, preservatives, alcohol, recreational drugs, pharmaceutical drugs and other causes. In the context of diet, gluten and plant toxins or plant defense mechanisms, are the primary drivers for gut inflammation. Meat does not cause intestinal degradation but regenerates the intestinal lining because of its bio-available protein and fats.

Intestinal degradation coincides with the corrosion of the micro villi responsible for nutrient absorption. As the damage accumulates, it leads to autoimmune diseases correlated with internal cysts, ulcers, intestinal inflammation, hair loss, skin problems, malnutrition, anemia, weakness, fatigue, sudden weight loss, constant bloat, skinny-fat figure, underdevelopment, bloody stools and diarrhea.

In adolescent children, acne is a primary symptom of intestinal damage and a compromised immune system. Acne is an autoimmune disorder. It is not a skin disorder. The genius and intelligence of the body forms boils on the face to signal to us that there is a serious disorder forming inside the body. Our intestinal lining protects us from the outside world just like our skin does. The degradation of our intestinal lining is akin to peeling off our external skin and exposing ourselves to our environment.

When gluten and other plant defense compounds puncture and leak past the gut, entering the blood stream, they cause a response from the immune system. Only plant foods have compounds and toxins which can damage and penetrate the gut lining. Meat does not. The body is not suppose to have foreign foods leaking through intestinal pipes and entering into the blood stream. When these foreign, plant food particles enter the body through the gut, they are bound to by immune cells and antibodies. The immune system attempts to arrest the invasion.

The body uses immunoglobulins or immune cells, to engage with foreign foods entering the blood stream undigested. Immune cells or antibodies tag the foreign foods in an attempt to neutralize and carry them away from the bloodstream, where they may cause oxidative damage to vital organs. Immune cells are proteins derived from lymphatic fluid which are rich in cholesterol and HDL. The immune system is reliant on the lymphatic system and it's fluids for all its defense mechanisms and antibodies.

The lymphatic system, it's fluids, it's immune cells, and antibodies, are highly dependent on cholesterol, saturated fat and HDL for proper building materials. This is important to note as in later chapters I will make the case that the modern populace and vegans are on a diet starving them of cholesterol and saturated fats, which are the primary nutrients needed for optimal human health. Special interest groups have indoctrinated youth and the medical establishment into believing that saturated fats and cholesterol should be avoided. Nothing is further from the truth. The immune system and lymphatic fluids depend upon cholesterol.

In healthy human beings, which are rare to find in the Modern West, lymphatic antibodies which bind to foreign foods are excreted in stool or urine within 24 hours. This is not too common today. The process is carried out in healthy human beings by the lymphatic systems. Antibodies travel in lymphatic fluid and into lymph nodes, where they may be further filtered and excreted through sweat or urine. Only sweat and urination through healthy kidneys can properly eliminate the foreign proteins bound to by antibodies from the immune system. The lymphatic system of the body is reliant on sweat and properly filtering kidneys for its detoxification processes.

Due to nutritional depravation and bodily degradation, these systems are handicapped and disabled in Modern Westerners. Instead, lymphatic antibodies and the foreign foods they have tagged, amalgamate and accumulate in the different lymphatic glands of the body. The lymphatic glands are primary storage sites for immune cells which have tagged foreign foods that have leaked through the gut, as well as dead cells, bacteria, metabolic waste, and modern environmental toxins, which are found in the body. When these catacombs of dead cells form to make protective pockets in and around lymph glands, the medical establishment calls it tumor.

To make matters worse, the armpits of the body which are able to perspire better than other parts of the skin, are clogged through the use of aluminum containing deodorants and anti-perspirants. This disables the armpits from being able to perspire and detox lymphatic glands near the breasts and thyroid. It is also one of the reasons today why women have such high incidence of breast cancer and thyroid problems. The lymph glands associated with the breast and thyroid are not able to perspire when the armpits are intentionally handicapped from performing their function.

Most people do not having properly functioning kidneys, livers, digestive tracts and skins. When these systems fail to function properly, the body resorts to the deposit of these foreign food particles and antibodies into the fatty tissues of the body's organs. This results in inflammation of different organs associated with different autoimmune disorders. The body will also attempt to deposit and excrete lymphatic fluids and antibodies in the lipids of facial skin cells. This is acne. The white puss in a pimple is lymphatic fluid. It is the same fluid found in tumors. **Primitive peoples have no such acne, despite lacking totally in dermatology, skin care regimens, antibacterial soaps, or facial cleansers. It is a non-issue because the diet is compatible with their physiology.**

Intestinally compromised individuals show different symptomatology depending on their genes. The most common initial symptoms across the board are facial acne, which develops in adolescence followed by hair loss. These are only signs of bodily degradation and premature aging due to diet and lifestyle, nothing more. The body is coming apart and aging rapidly. This is essentially what autoimmune diseases are.

As individuals lose further body integrity, the diseases and degenerative processes become more severe causing autoimmune disorders, such as rheumatoid arthritis, hypo or hyper thyroidism, Hashimoto's thyroiditis, celiac disease, crohn's disease etc. When foreign food particles which leak through the gut deposit into the fatty tissue of the brain, they produce symptoms of mental illness, foggy thinking, memory loss, and all other degenerative conditions associated with the brain.

The medical establishment asserts that autoimmune disorders are a condition where the body's immune system mistakenly attacks itself. They place the blame on "faulty genes". This is wrong thinking. A small seed has imbued within it the infinite intelligence of nature, to be able to survive and defend itself to the best of its ability. It requires a deep disconnect from nature to believe in such absurdities, such as the body attacking itself, or killing itself through it's own genetic shortcomings.

Fortunately, there are many brilliant physicians who are independent thinkers and acknowledge just how preposterous main-stream medical thinking is. Our current medical paradigm and way of thinking, of blaming diseases on genes, is equivalent to The European Dark Ages, where diseases were blamed on witchcraft and black magic. The public is placed on an anti-human diet, but when disorders manifest, the blame is placed on a questionable gene passed down from some distant ancestor. It is an easy way to scapegoat problems to an invisible enemy.

During The Dark Ages in Europe, there were thousands of cases where farm animals such as cows, were put on trial for causing diseases to people in the town by way of black magic. Cows were put on trial and their verdicts were decided depending on how they "moo'd" in court. If a cow was found guilty of black magic, it was hung in the town center. Never under-estimate human stupidity and most importantly, do not believe that we are today at the peak of our spiritual, intellectual, creative or physical evolution. There has been an involution of the human species, not an evolution. To convey this idea would require several volumes of work which I cannot even begin to touch here.

There is nothing in nature which attacks itself. Everything in nature strives to survive, from bacteria, plants, animals and yes, even the human body. The human body has inherent, intrinsic intelligence. There are innumerable number of functions, enzymatic reactions and metabolic processes, carried out by the body without our active participation. It is a miracle of life. In our growth and development, our sole responsibility is to obtain and consume nutrition. The body is responsible for digestion, absorption, elimination, and production of new bodily tissues. It is the intelligence of the female body which is able to develop and give a new life. It is not the hubris and arrogance of man which drives all these miracles of life.

Because of the deleterious effects gluten and plant toxins have on the gut, one could assume that those who are suffering from skin issues, autoimmune related hair loss or any of the assortment of autoimmune disorders, do indeed have micro villi atrophy or leaky gut. These individuals are not only challenging their immune system with every morsel of plant food but also can not digest and absorb any nutrients. **If they are on vegan diets, there are absolutely no nutrients which can help to replenish and restore intestinal lining.** The gut lining is made of flesh, of protein and fat, not of kale and spinach. Those on the Standard American Diet with 5 to 11 servings of grains per day do not fare much better.

The challenge with leaky gut and micro villi atrophy, is that even if one consumes a diet high in nutrient-dense animals foods or proper supplements based on animal foods, they may not be able to absorb them. Fat-soluble vitamins such as A, D and K2 come together in nutrient-dense animal foods. Individuals with damaged gut linings will experience nausea and fatigue after consuming fatty animal foods. These people can only digest sugar. Severe Vitamin D deficiency is very common across the country. One could assume that if an individual is deficient in D, they are also deficient in A, K2, most minerals, and B vitamins, because these foods come together in the natural world. Leaky gut and micro villi atrophy cause severe starvation of nearly every single mineral and vitamin.

To say that all autoimmune diseases are caused by gluten and plant toxins would be wrong. **My argument is that gluten, modern-wheat and over-reliance on plants, are some of the primary contributors to the development of autoimmune diseases, premature aging and bodily degradation.** There are many other contributing factors to autoimmune disease, such as drugs, both recreational and pharmaceutical, environmental toxins such as mercury, agricultural chemicals and pesticides, and finally psychological stress. However, it would not be wrong to state that individuals who are interested in health, development, and longevity, would benefit immensely with the removal of modern, improperly prepared wheat and plants from the diet. It could perhaps be the single best and most easy lifestyle change one could make.

For those who insist on consuming some form of bread, I would advise to make your own. Source organic traditional grains such as Einkorn Wheat. Soak them for 24 hours, grind them to a flour, and ferment them for a day or two with a proper yeast culture. Further, make sure to consume your breads with adequate amounts of animal fats such as butter or cream-cheese. This makes the bread far more digestible. Many health food stores such as Whole-Foods now offer sourdough breads which are prepared in the traditional artisan way, and are far more healthy than the commercially produced breads found in aisles of grocers.

CHAPTER 4

Fruit-Sugar, Premature Aging & Disease

Of all the plant foods which have little to no nutritional value, it was the study and understanding of fruit which had shocked me most. Fruits are often portrayed as innocent, colorful foods, with a wide range of health benefits and antioxidants. The fruit of modernity are in fact one of the least healthy, whole-foods available. Vegan diets are subject to abnormally high amounts of fruit consumption due to their exclusion of animal foods.

In The Standard American Diet, most packaged, processed, and refined foods, have their fat calories removed and replaced with calories from sugar in the form of high fructose corn syrup. Fructose is the predominant sugar found in fruits and sweet vegetables such as carrots and beets. Most refined and processed foods are sweetened using the very same type of sugar found in all fruits.

My own experiments with diets high in fruits were extremely deleterious to say the least. I can say without a doubt, large amounts of fruit are one of the worse dietary recommendations I have ever experienced. Of all the vegans, it is the so called fruitarians who seem to age and degenerate the worse. There are many cases of not only individuals on the internet, but also communes collectively partaking in experimental fruit-based diets, with extremely devastating consequences. To understand why fruit and fructose are so devastating to health, I must elaborate on the history of fruit cultivation, and how fruit sugar is metabolized by the body. There is strong science pointing to fruit sugar exasperating every single disease known to man.

Domestication and Cultivation of Wild Edible Fruit

The fruit of today on average contain 30 times more sugar than their wild, ancestral progenitors. The fruit found in supermarkets and groceries in the industrial world are unnatural, hybridized foods, that are not found in wild nature. In wild nature, we find low-sugar, bitter and starchy fruits, which are only available in the fall. Fruit is not available year-round like it is today with the advent of global trade.

Animals and hunter-gatherer cultures used the abundance of ripe, low-sugar fruit available in the fall, to put on fat for the winter when food was scarce. We see this in many animals such as bears, which gorge on wild berries in the fall and go into hibernation during winter. The extra fat reserves offers them slow, steady fuel, which can be used for energy during hibernation.

Most often, the fruits available were wild berries. In fact, most modern fruits such as apples, plums and watermelons, resembled small berries prior to their hybridization by man. They were amongst some of the digestible wild fruits. Majority of wild fruits in nature are consumed by birds as they are far too starchy and seedy for human consumption. Many are also poisonous. There are no poisonous meat foods.

Over generations, farmers and breeders grew fruit trees in highly controlled environments, where they could manage cross pollination and select desired traits for the next generation of fruit. The traits desired for fruits were less seeds, more sweet or sugar, and less starchy fiber. Breeders would plant the seeds from the sweetest fruits and burn or discard of those seeds from fruits which did not have the desired traits.

This hybridization process has been repeated now for hundreds of generations, since the very begging of human agriculture. The accumulation of this hybridization process, has today provided the world with the year round availability of high-sugar fruits in all seasons. This is totally unprecedented in the history of natural evolution. I will outline a few of the most common fruits consumed today which bear almost no resemblance to their ancestral progenitors. This is by no means a comprehensive expose.

Each and every grocery store fruit is genetically altered through the hybridization process. Processes which could have never occurred naturally on their own. In nature, seeds which carry on the genetic material for the next generation, are those which are the strongest and most fit to survive. Breeders have for hundreds of generations artificially manipulated this process by selecting seeds based on the fruit's sugar content.

Peach was originally domesticated in China around 4000 BC. It's ancestral progenitor was very small and resembled a cherry. It had very thick, waxy, inedible skin with a large seed. The taste was described as salty and earthy, alluding to the starchy fiber content of the fruit. Only half of the flesh was edible with the rest being too fibrous. The modern peach has very soft skin, is 64 times larger, with 90% edible flesh and with a much smaller seed.

Wild Banana is very different from the yellow sugar bombs available in groceries today. It's progenitor was very starchy, stalky, full of seeds, and virtually inedible. The modern banana has no seeds, very low starch and fiber, with 30 times more sugar. When I write that these fruits were starchy and not sweet, think of a potato. That is starchy.

Watermelon was first recorded to have been harvested 5,000 years ago in ancient Egypt. The original watermelons were two inches in diameter, extremely bitter, full of seeds, stalky and mostly inedible. The modern watermelon has been cultivated to be seedless or with very little seed,1500 times larger, and with 60 times more sugar than its progenitor.

Pineapple is native to Central America and cultivated in tropical regions of the western hemisphere. It's wild variety is about the size of a small apple. When ripe, its fiber is stalky and inedible raw. The raw fruit is extremely acidic and can burn the throat, tongue and lips. Traditionally, they were used to tenderize meats and also for medicinal purposes, but not as a food.

Citrus fruits in nature are small, sour and acidic. Contact with most wild lime can cause rashes, burns or blisters on the skins of sensitive individuals. Traditionally, they were used to tenderize meats as well as seasoning. They were not used as a food, except for obtaining small amounts of structured water to hydrate with.

The fruits available year-round in grocery stores are not found in the wild. It is only in recent human history, that fruits have become available year-round, due to hybridization of cultivates and globalization. Many of the fruits are cross breeds between different species of fruits. For example, a pluot is a cross between a plum and an apricot. A tangelo is a cross between tangerine and grapefruit. The results of seed breeding are tasty, high sugar, edible fruit. Although the abundant supply of fruit may seem like a great innovation for mankind, the science and the facts regarding fruit sugar tell a different story.

Fructose and Disease

Dr. Robert Lustig is an American pediatric endocrinologist and a professor emeritus of Pediatrics Division of Endocrinology at University of California, San Francisco, where he specializes in neuroendocrinology and childhood obesity. Dr. Lustig came to public attention in 2009 after one of his public lectures, *Sugar: The Bitter Truth,* became popular on youtube. Another one titled, *The Most Destructive force in The Universe: Sugar -A Global Pandemic,* was just as superb.

Dr. Robert Lustig's research examines the links between consumption of fructose, the primary sugar found in fruit, honey, some vegetables, and most processed foods, and the development of metabolic syndrome. Degenerative diseases included in metabolic syndrome include type 2 diabetes, high blood pressure, cardiovascular disease, non-alcoholic fatty liver disease, obesity, and much more. Dr. Lustig argues that the liver is damaged by the fructose in fruit juice, vegetable juice, table sugar, and high fructose corn syrup, that is added to packaged and processed market foods.

The chemistry of all types of sugars such as sucrose, fructose and glucose, are identical, but nearly all the studies done on the subject of sugars show that fructose is in fact the most harmful to the body. The specific problems we find with fructose is the way it is metabolized by the body as opposed to glucose, protein and fat. Fructose is only metabolized by the liver and not regulated by insulin, therefore it can not be used by the muscles of the body, or stored as muscle glycogen. Fructose also can not be used by the brain or other organs for fuel. The body is only able to use glucose from starches or fats from animal food for fuel, not fructose from sugar.

When fructose is consumed, the body must convert it to liver fat or it will flow in the blood stream and become a free-radical. The body initially tries to rid itself of fructose by directing it immediately to the liver for removal, just the same way the body deals with alcohol, however, the liver is only able to process about 25 grams of fructose. One modern banana has 30 grams of fructose.

The body does not allow the glands, organs, brain or muscle, to use fructose as fuel. The body perceives fruit-sugar as poison and seeks to get rid of it. Due to high amounts of sugar found in modern fruits, the liver is overburdened every time a high sugar fruit is consumed. The excess sugars from fruit float around in the blood stream, causing oxidative stress, killing cells, damaging organs, glycating cells, and oxygen depletion.

Glycation and oxidative stress from sugars rapidly age and destroy cells in every single organ of the body, including the skin. Glycation is the process whereby sugars unnaturally bind to proteins and fats of cells, causing damage. Wrinkles form when sugars glycate and damage skin cells. Glycation also occurs inside the body, damaging and aging organs.

Sugars path of destruction may initially start by degrading organs and causing organ stress, but it's effects cascade into systemic disease, degenerative breakdown, and premature aging. The excess sugars that are not metabolized by the liver cause gut-dysbiosis and candida overgrowth in the gut. Fungus and candida grow in response to excess sugars. These microorganisms are opportunistic pathogens which spawn in a compromised, sugar-laden body.

Acids and alcohol fermentation in the gut are byproducts of candida and fungus sugar metabolism. The consequence of these organisms fermenting sugars in the gut, results in a myriad of skin issues including but not limited to acne, dandruff, psoriasis, and eczema. When the fungus or candida become systemic in the body and blood in response to high blood sugars, the body enters a state of low oxygen, breeding an environment for tumors to develop and grow. In addition fruit-sugar feeding pathogenic candida and fungus, tumors or cancer cells consume 15 times more fruit-sugar than do other cells in the body.

"Depriving cancer cells of sugar, activates a metabolic pathway and signaling amplification loop, that leads to cancer cell death as a result of the toxic effect of reactive oxygen species." -Journal of Molecular System Biology 6/26/2012 Gracher and Colleagues Data

"Cancer are so sensitive to sugar supply, that cutting the supply will suppress the disease." -German Cancer Institute, Rainer Klement, Ulrike Kammerer

In 1924 Nobel laureate Dr. Otto Warburg MD, wrote a paper on the metabolism of tumors. He clearly defined that the fermentation of sugars in metabolism replaces oxygen and provokes mutagenic effects. He states "Cancer growth is caused when cancer convert glucose into energy without using oxygen". Otto Warburg won a Nobel prize for his findings.

"Numerous important findings show that cancer cells can readily metabolize fructose to increase proliferation. This has major significance for cancer patients given dietary fructose consumption, which indicates that efforts to reduce refined fructose or inhibit fructose- mediations actions will disrupt cancer growth."- *UCLA Johnson Comprehensive Cancer Center*

"It has been known been known since 1923 that tumor cells use far more glucose than normal cells."-
Huntsman Cancer Institute

One of the most revealing ways oncologist find cancer in the body is by employing a pet scan after injecting sugar into the blood stream. When sugar is injected into the blood stream, the cancer cells devour the sugar. Given that cancer cells utilize sugar 15 times more than normal cells, it is easy to find the epicenter of the cancer and where it is metastasizing towards. Ayer, Ph.D., Professor in the Department of Oncological Sciences and Graber Ph.D., Professor of Molecular and Medical Pharmacology, investigated the metabolism of sugar and found that there are biochemical signals present in cancer cells that attract and utilize these sugars to perpetuate malignancy.

Data on Fruit from Vegan Communities

It is ironic that the most damning evidence against fruit comes from those who are considered veteran health authorities in the vegan community. Two of the most prominent vegan authorities are Dr. Gabriel Cousens MD and Brian Clement Ph.D., L.N.. With their combined experience, they have over 70 years of working with hundreds of thousands of people. After decades of research, both have concluded that fruit should be excluded from the diet of anyone who is combatting disease or interested in longevity. Although I am not in a

Brian Clement is the director of the world oldest natural health institute, The Hippocrates Health Institute. Hippocrates Health Institute itself is one of the finest institutes in the world, attracting the most new and advanced health technologies. Working with hundreds of thousands of people, he has seen first hand what works and does not work when combatting disease and aging. He has been involved with the institute for over 50 years.

When he first joined Hippocrates Health Institute in the 70's, they advocated for sugars in the form of raw of foods such as carrot juice, mangoes, and other fruits. Over the years, they found that when sugars where removed from the diets of their patients, they got better, and would regress when reintroducing fruit into the diet. They found that fruits enhanced every single degenerative disease they were presented with. Brian Clement has a profound lecture available on youtube titled *Sugar: The Kiss of Death,* where he speaks about The Institute's experiences with fruit in the diets of their patients.

"Please heed on this one. Know that I'm not a genius research scientist but I'm a nutritionist and I have been one so my entire adult life, and after I came to this conclusion at Hippocrates more than 30 years ago and we removed fruit from the diet of people who were facing major diseases, and our medical team has clearly and clearly observed, that they have greatly improved verses when they continue to eat fruits."
-Brian Clement PhD., L.N., Director of Hippocrates Health Institute

All forms of sugar, wether it be from refined sugar or unnatural fruit, perpetuate inflammation through out the body, leading to the development of metastases of every form of cancer. Sugar also causes mineral excretion through urine. The demineralization process that many vegans go through is profound. It is occurring as well in most Americans on The Standard American Diet, but happening exponentially faster in vegans, particular those who consume large amounts of fruit.

The fruit itself, even if grown in the highest quality soil, can not concentrate enough minerals or nutrients needed for human health. Not even a fraction. Due to the high sugar content and corresponding stress it places on the body, the fruits cause the body to excrete vitamin and mineral reserves in order to deal with stress of sugar metabolism.

A list of diseases associated with sugar are:

- Chronic Fatigue syndrome.
- Chrohns disease, leaky gut, diverticulosis.
- Candida, fungus, yeast.
- Acne, roseacea, psoriasis, eczema.
- ALS, parkinsons, MS, alzheimers.
- Mental illness, bipolar disorder, ADD, brain fog.
- Infertility, impotence, sterility.
- Premature aging and nutrient deficiencies.

"Studies have shown that consuming excessive quantities of sugar such as sucrose and high fructose corn syrup cause a large urinary calcium excretion increase, both in healthy study subjects and in those who were prone to kidney stones. This is not surprising since sugar is a highly acidifying food." -Lawoyin, S.[5]

Dr. Gabrel Cousens M.D. is the director of The Tree of Life Health Institute. He has over 40 years experience using plant-based nutritional interventions in diet and disease. He is also an advocate for minimizing sugar and fruit in the diet and has come to the same conclusion as Brian Clement Ph.D. He states in a video available on youtube titled, *is 100% fruit diet healthy?- Dr. Gabriel Cousens,*

"We have seen the most danger, in my 40 years, I've seen the most bad stories on fruit-based diets...

---

[5] Bone mineral content in patients with calcium urolithiasis. S Lawoyin, S Sismilich, R Browne, C Y Pak. 1979 Dec 28.

There have been two major fruitarian communities...that have attempted (to sustain themselves on fruit), after one year women stopped having their period, people became mentally imbalanced and it was a pretty big disaster. The person running that, Johnny Lovelace became paralyzed from the legs down. It was a total failure. Women couldn't reproduce."-Dr. Gabriel Cousens M.D.

"The 2nd study was in Australia, it was by another natural hygienist person and it lasted 3 years...but what happen was the person running it stopped it because he had ethics. He could only go so far and what do you see, women can't reproduce or if they do reproduce their children had far more mental deficiencies, far more mental retardation." -*Dr. Gabriel Cousens M.D.*

"The problem with sugar and its a big problem, is that, fructose is 10 times more active as a glycosylation agent. Which means it creates free radicals, it combines unnaturally with the lipids and the proteins and inflames the glia cells of the brain. It ultimately creates problems in the body that aren't good. We also know that cancer cells needs 10 to 50 times more glucose or fructose. If you have cancer you don't want to be having a lot of fruit because it can aggravate it." - Dr. Gabriel Cousens M.D.

"The people who live the longest are the ones that eat lowest sugar including fruit."- Dr. Gabriel Cousens M.D.

There was an amazing study done called, *The Nurse Study,* performed over the coarse of 15 years on nurses. The study found that participants who took in 25% or more of their daily calories from sugar, were more than twice as likely to die from heart disease as those diets that included less than 10% added sugar overall. The odds of dying of heart disease rose in tandem with the portion or percentage of sugar and carbohydrates in the diet, and that was true regardless of sex, physical activity level, and body mass index.

Plant-based eaters and vegans do not obtain fat-soluble vitamins and cholesterol from their diet, which are needed as building blocks to build neurotransmitters, hormones and healthy cellular turn-over. The restriction of these foods from their diets, force them to replace the calories with sugar. If you remove animal foods from the diet, you are only left with plants, which all contain varying degrees of sugars. Every plant food breaks down to sugar.

Vegans, plant-based pundits and majority on the Standard American Diet, are subject to constant blood-sugar spikes throughout the day. It is important to understand, that every vegan food breaks down to a sugar. All plants are carbohydrates and store their energy in the form of sugar, as opposed to animals that store energy as fat.

Vegans and plant-based health authorities argue that fruit is mankind's original food and full of nutrition. That fruit requires no hunting, no cooking, taste good and can be picked from the tree. It appeals to sentiment and emotions. The argument is absolutely void when challenged with the science of fructose metabolism and the history of fruit cultivation. In the wild today, it would be impossible to sustain and live on fruit, anywhere in the world. The sweet, sugar-rich, calorically-dense fruits of modernity, do not exist in nature. Desert, forest, mountains or tropics, you will only be able to sustain yourself by hunting wild animals. Foraging wild plants would only offer limited sustenance, not enough to survive.

US Sugar Consumption Year 1850-2000, Grams Per Day

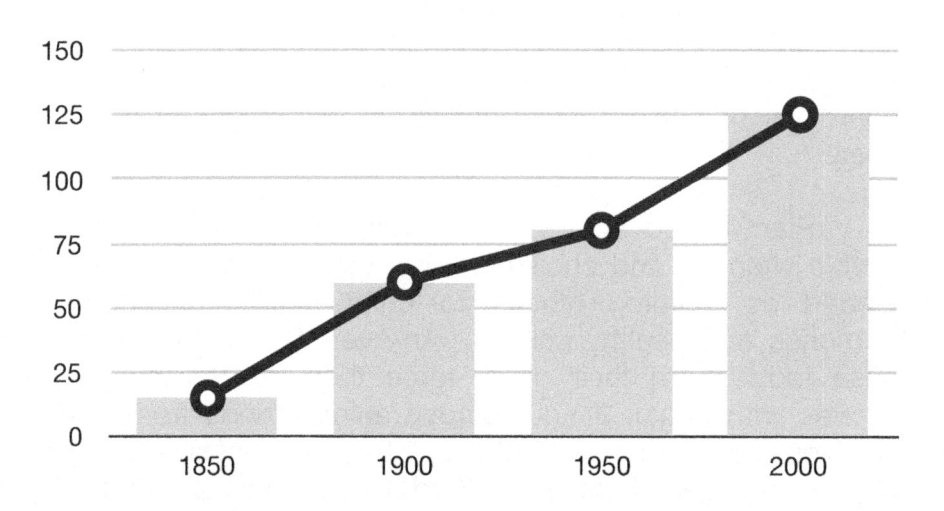

The idea that fruit should be included for it's antioxidant qualities is also erroneous. It is due to sheer ignorance. The greatest antioxidant is cholesterol which can be found in cholesterol rich foods. The corrosive sugar in fruit causes far more oxidative damage then could ever be worth its antioxidant content. The antioxidant quantity is pathetic when compared to animals foods and their protective, healing, and regenerating effects on human cells.

"Your health and likely your lifespan will be determined by the proportion of fat versus sugar you burn over a lifetime."-Dr. Ron Rosedale

In the Standard American Diet, nearly all packaged and processed foods, soft drinks and sodas, are sweetened using high fructose corn syrup. It is essentially the same sugar found in fruit and is the primary driver of disease and metabolic syndrome in the United States. The current U.S. annual consumption of fructose is 63 pounds per person, in vegans, it is far higher.

Originally, fructose was very scarce, only available in the form of honey. However with the advent of the sugar cane industry, hybrid fruit, and globalization, sugar became a global commodity. Sugar consumption has skyrocketed over the last 200 years. If we examine the dietary trend over the last 170 years, we see that sugar from all sources has steadily gained a more prominent role in the diet. The increase of sugar and removal of animal foods from the diet are direct correlates to the modern degenerative disease endemic. It is absurd to believe that the animal foods we have been consuming since the dawn of our species are the cause of our diseases. See the graph from U.S. Commerce Service and USDA.

Data from U.S. Commerce Service 1822-1910 and Economic Research Service USDA 1910-2010

The sugar found in fruit and the sugar found in processed foods such as soda, are no different and act the same way in the body. Biochemically they are the exact same. The science, the data, the facts, and the anecdotal evidence all point towards fruit-sugar causing harm to human physiology. The body does have a limited need for sugar but not in the form found in fruits nor the quantity.

Traditional cultures obtained daily sugar or carbohydrate in the form of glucose, not fructose. Glucose is found in starchy foods such as rice, beans, potatoes and breads. Glucose was obtained by fermenting and properly preparing starchy grains such as sourdough bread. Another example is the use of white rice and milling by oriental cultures. White rice is essentially rice which has been milled, which removes the husk and bran layers. The husk and bran layers, or outer shell of the seed, contain the anti-nutrients, plant biochemicals and defense mechanisms intrinsic to the rice plant. When the outer layers of the seed are removed, you are left with a fairly digestible, white kernel of rice, which offers pure glucose, not fructose. These were intelligently prepared carbohydrate additions to cuisines which were centered on nutrient-dense, high fat, animal foods.

In summary I wish to emphasize that fruit was only available in the fall. These were typically berries and other low-sugar fruits. Animals and humans would gorge on these fruits in order to put on fat for the coming winter months. They were a seasonal addition to the diet. Today, these fruit sugars or fructose, play a predominant role in the diet of Americans and vegans. Most so called "health foods" have their fat calories and corresponding fat-soluble vitamins removed, and replaced instead with sugar in the form of high fructose corn syrup. This practice is rampant in many low-fat diary products.

Furthermore, removing animal foods from the diet, invariably leads to replacing those calories with sugars, which are totally lacking in nutrition. Every plant breaks down into sugar when digested. Sugar or plant-based diets have been a profound contributor to the physical and mental degradation of The American People.

CHAPTER 5

Animals foods vs Plant Foods Nutrient Composition

The information regarding plant and fruit toxicity and their corresponding detrimental effects on human physiology may come as a surprise to many people. There are those who believe that subsisting on a vegan diet are worth the supposed health benefits and nutritional content, regardless of the plant toxins and issues with sugars. The problem is, the idea of plant-based or vegan nutrition is a myth, totally unfounded in scientific literature. They contain no sort of vitamins and minerals needed for human development and growth.

The word vitamin itself originated from the the latin "vita", to give life, as in vital or vitality. Vitamins are a wide spectrum of organic substances that are necessary for normal health and growth in the higher forms of animal life. Vitamins in general are of a catalytic nature, whereby they facilitate chemical reactions to take place in the body's cells. In order for the body's cells to perform certain functions, vitamins must be present.

I wish to emphasize, that yes, plants such as potatoes can fuel you with healthy carbs, yes, fresh vegetable juices can hydrate and offer electrolytes, yes, plants can offer fiber, but they do not build or give strength to the mind or body. They do not have the sort of vitamins, minerals, or most other class of nutrients, which develop the body and mind.

Vitamins are classified into two groups, water-soluble and fat-soluble. The distinction between the two is important in regards to nutrient composition of animal and plant foods. Fat-soluble vitamins are found exclusively in animal fat. Plants do not contain any fat-soluble vitamins. Fat-soluble vitamins are stored in the fat of humans and animals.

Water-soluble vitamins are of liquid nature, do not store in the body for long periods, and must be replenished often. Water-soluble vitamins are found in the highest concentration in animal blood, bloody organs, muscle meats, milks, and egg yolks. Plant juices have very few of the water-soluble vitamins and in very small concentrations, not enough to support human life.

It is significant to consider the fact that plants come with intrinsic anti-nutrients which inhibit absorption of nutrients. This, in conjunction with the relatively low levels of any nutrients, make them wholly improper for growth, development and nourishment. They are secondary additions to a healthy diet.

Fat-soluble vitamins are Vitamins A, D, E, K and P. Water-soluble vitamins are the B family of vitamins and vitamin C. The development process of human beings and growth of the brain, requires large amounts of fat-soluble vitamins A, D and K, as well as large amounts of water-soluble B vitamins. The lack of these vitamins causes improper development of the skull, resulting in long narrow faces, narrow dental arches, crowding of the teeth, dental cavities and smaller brains.

Vegan diets are utterly lacking in these nutrients, so much so that there is a "vegan look", once you understand what you are looking for. The importance of these nutrients were first discovered by Dr. Weston A. Price DDS, in the early 1900's and recorded in his monumental work, *Nutrition and Physical Degeneration*.

This book would be incomplete without paying homage to The Great Weston A. Price. A great portion of the nutritional thesis of this books rests on his work and builds on top of it. Dr. Price was a Canadian born dentist known for his theories regarding nutrition, dental health, physical health and physical development. He founded the National Dental Association of which he was the chairman from 1914-1928.

After many years as a successful dentist and pulling out tens of thousands of teeth, Dr. Price decided to travel the world and search for primitive, isolated, and "savage" tribes, in order to learn of how they dealt with dental cavities. What he found was that dental cavities and crowding teeth were nearly non-existent in any of these isolated, non-industrialized cultures. He attributed there splendid growth and development, as well as superb health, to nutritional and dietary factors present in their nutrient rich, animal-based diets. He recorded his work in his Magnus Opus, *Nutrition and Physical Degeneration.* The book was one of the most enjoyable I have ever had the pleasure of reading, and is replete with photos of the people he studied.

His book details his ethnographical nutritional studies spanning diverse cultures including Native Americans, Pygmies, Australian Aborigines, The Lotschental of Switzerland, Polynesians, The Pathans of India, Eskimo, Quichua Indians of the High Andes, amongst many others. He found across the board, that as long as people remained on their indigenous diets, they remained in great health, developed strong bodies, full dental arches, large broad faces, large skulls, and were virtually immune to dental cavities, as well as the degenerative diseases of modern industrialized peoples. The common factor all of their respective diets had were nutrient-dense animal foods high in fat-soluble vitamins and minerals.

There were cultures who ate only meat, some who consumed only meat and milk, and other who consumed meat and plants, but none who consumed only plants. What is of most significant is the emphasis each culture placed on obtaining nutrient-dense animal foods which they understood to insure them of healthy births and proper development of their children.

Upon testing the nutrient and mineral content of their food, he found, that that they had on average 10-30 times more nutrition than the food of western commerce. At his time in the 1920's, North America was facing issues of depleted soils. Dr. Price often commented on the physical appearance of the primitives and called them "splendid specimens", and described their teeth as two rows of pearls. The book is filled with pictures of his documentations and is amongst the most objective body of work ever done on nutritional sciences.

There are those who may argue that the people he documented had splendid health, teeth and physical development due to genes. This is wrong, as he also documents many different families with siblings from a single household. The siblings who had moved away from their indigenous lands and into commercialized cities and towns in nearby areas, subsisted off of the foods of modernity. These foods being white sugar, packaged fruits, jams, jellies, flours, canned beans, and vegetables. All of them suffered from extreme dental decay, physical degeneration, and disease very similar to what we find in The West. The diets of these siblings were essentially vegan and Standard American. Those siblings who remained on the indigenous land and consumed their ancestral diet, had splendid health. Teeth did not decay even though they did not utilize any type of oral hygiene.

To emphasize on the nutritional deprivation occurring at present state in America, I want the readers to think of everyone they know who has needed the cosmetic aid of orthodontist and dentist. It is widespread across the population. Orthodontist serve to cosmetically patch up deformed dental arches and crowded teeth. The deformed dental arches and crowding of teeth are a consequence of improper skull development. When the human body does not receive proper nutrition in its developmental years, the skull does not develop and mature properly. The consequence is smaller brains, smaller skulls, and crowded teeth. The deformities percolate into the rest of the skeletal and glandular system as well.

Dentist serve by pulling out or severing the nerves of decaying teeth and replacing them with amalgams or dentures. Without the aid of these modern cosmetics, most of modern people would be walking around with crowded, decaying teeth. The pain would be unbearable for many of us to handle. Our poor oral health is indicative of our nutritional deprivation.

The prevalence of crowded or decaying teeth, and narrow faces, have consequences beyond mere cosmetics. Our brains are literally shrinking with each passing generation. The reduced skull size has an extremely detrimental effect on the brain, stunting psychological growth and maturation. The details of starving, malnourished, and stunted brains, I will elaborate on in a later chapter.

Although Dr. Price found many tribes who subsisted off of both animal and plant foods, he found none who subsisted on plant foods alone. He did find several that subsisted off of meat alone and were in superb health, such as the Eskimo. Furthermore, he found that each and every single tribe had animal foods which they highly prized for it's nutrient and life giving properties. These people knew that without the animal foods they would not prosper. Often times, they would go to great lengths to obtain these nutrient-dense animal foods.

The Lotschental people of Switzerland held so sacred and dear their butter, that they would often put a wick in a block of butter and use it a candle in local churches. This was used as a symbolic gesture. They would pray and give thanks to God for their butter and acknowledged the health giving properties inherent in it. They also consumed properly prepared sourdough bread. The grain for the bread was grown in nutrient rich, glacial soils. It was also prepared in the traditional artisan way which made it more digestible. The bread was always drenched in butter and was primarily used as a vehicle for obtaining more fat-soluble vitamins in the diet.

Dr. Price observed that tribes and peoples who did not have access to domesticated cattle for dairy consumption, obtained nutrition from the nose to tail consumption of animals. When an animal was killed, they went straight for the fatty organs and bone marrow. Often times, organs such as the liver were consumed raw. Liver was considered a sacred superfood in every single traditional and primitive culture around the world. Certain tribes in Africa would not even touch the liver with their hands but extract it from the body of the animal and consume it using sticks. This act of not using their bare hands was a way of paying homage to the animal and it's liver, which they considered sacred. The following is a chart comparing the nutrient content of apples, carrots, red muscle meat and beef liver.

	BEEF LIVER (100G)	RED MEAT (100G)	CARROT (100G)	APPLE (100G)
CALIUM	11.0 mg	11.0 mg	3.3 mg	3.0 mg
PHOSPHORUS	476.0 mg	140.0 mg	31.0 mg	6.0 mg
MAGNESIUM	18.0 mg	15.0 mg	6.2 mg	5.0 mg
POTASSIUM	380. mg	370.0 mg	222.0 mg	139.0 mg
IRON	8.8 mg	3.3 mg	.6 mg	.1 mg
ZINC	4.0 mg	4.4 mg	.3 mg	.05 mg
COPPER	12.0 mg	.18 mg	.08 mg	.04 mg
VITAMIN B12	111.0 mcg	2.0 mcg	None	None
BIOTIN	95.0 mcg	2.0 mcg	.4 mcg	None
FOLIC ACID	8.0 mcg	4.0 mcg	20.0 mcg	7.0 mcg
VITAMIN B6	.03 mg	.1 mg	.10 mg	.03 mg
PANTOTHENIC ACID	9.9	.42 mg	.19 mg	.11 mg
NIACIN	16.5 mg	4.0 mg	.60 mg	.10 mg
RIBOFLAVIN	4.0 mg	.20 mg	.05 mg	.02 mg
THIAMIN	.25 mg	.05 mg	.05 mg	.02 mg
VITAMIN A	50,000 IU	400 IU	NONE	NONE
VITAMIN D	20 IU	10 IU	NONE	NONE
VITAMIN E	.6 mg	2.0 mg	.1 mg	.4 mg
VITAMIN C	27.0 mg	None	6.0 mg	7.0 mg

Plants contain very little of some of the necessary nutrients needed for optimal health, but lack in the majority of nutrients needed for human well-being, growth and development. The lack of these nutrients cause immense pain and suffering aside from just improper development and growth. The absence of just one vitamin handicaps specific metabolic reactions in cells and imbalances the entire body. Some of the fat-soluble vitamins which are exclusive to mammalian tissue, form biological membranes and are crucial to maintaining the integrity and structure of the body. Without these fat-soluble vitamins, not only will the body not develop properly, but crucial systems such as digestive lining, organs, and eyes, begin to break down prematurely.

Vitamins, Minerals their Functions and Food Sources

In wild nature, foods contain many or most of the nutrients needed in proper proportions and come as a package. Isolated vitamins and minerals do not exist as they do in synthetic supplementation. Synthetic or food-based supplementation are at best crutches but can never replace the role of whole-food nutrition. Plant-based multivitamins are a joke and should not be considered. They do not have enough nutrition and come with a host of anti-nutrients which again inhibit their proper absorption.

In real foods, vitamins and minerals have an innumerable number of cofactors which assist with their absorption and utilization by the body. Nonetheless, it is absolutely crucial that individuals seeking to improve their health utilize supplements for a time. They are not necessary year round, but may be required in times of extreme stress, or when first undergoing the "development process", or when dealing with a disease. They are indispensable for autoimmune and gastrointestinal compromised individuals who have difficulty digesting and absorbing foods.

Their use can greatly speed up developmental and regenerative processes. Further, most foods and bodies are extremely devoid of needed vitamins and minerals due to modern farming practices. The bodies are starved and consuming only nutrient-dense foods are not enough. The body needs assistance and a kickstarter. Synthetics supplements are often far better than plant-based supplements, due to natural anti-nutrient and inhibitory factors present in plant fibers. Synthetic supplementation is also able to concentrate higher amounts of vitamins. I should stress here again, supplements are not meant to be taken for life, but only for a time. They come with their own side effects which I will go into some detail later.

Vitamin A is one of the most important nutrients needed for human health. It is one of the most common deficiencies today, and its deficiency is very prevalent in vegans and vegetarians. Vitamin A builds, strengthens and supports epithelial cells, which make up the mucous membrane of the body, intestinal lining, and the skin. Mucous membranes are essentially the internal skin of the body. Vitamin A is crucial for rebuilding the gut-lining of individuals suffering from autoimmune diseases and leaky gut. Without Vitamin A from real animal foods, it is impossible to rebuild the gut lining. It is also necessary for proper bone, skull and brain development. Supplemental sources of Vitamin A are cod liver oils.

Food sources of Vitamin A are butter, eggs, and organ meats. Vegetables do not contain any vitamin A. Youth are often told that plants contain beta-carotene which can substitute for vitamin A. Nothing can be further from the truth. Beta-carotene is a plant pigment. Beta-carotene is a precursor to vitamin A, and it's conversion to vitamin A can only be accomplished by the digestive tracts of herbivores and ruminant animals. I will elaborate more on the digestive tract of humans and herbivores in the chapter.

Low Vitamin A is the leading cause of macular degeneration, blindness, skin problems, poor immunity, and accumulation of beta-amyloid plaque in the brain associated with Alzheimers disease.

I will quote here again veteran vegan nutritionist and Dr. Gabreil Cousens. The words of this man can not be undervalued as he is amongst those who have practiced and worked with a vegan diet for decades, not only on himself but on tens of thousands of patients. This is not a man who became a vegan yesterday and self proclaimed nutritional expert today. Of all the vegan doctors, he has the highest level of integrity and admits where there are short comings. Heed his words in regards to the short comings of vegan diets.

"Vitamin A is actually hard for vegans to get because its not that available. You say what about beta-carotene, but the conversion rate from beta-carotene into retinol which is the active form of Vitamin A isn't that great. 23-47% conversion rate. But 9% of people don't really convert at all. So thats a problem with vitamin A. But vitamin A is needed for a lot of functions. One of the most important functions is the lining of the intestines where you get the IGGA, which is a whole immune protective system, so thats one piece thats really important. Obviously its good for your skin, its good for different things, but its a problem, not everybody is able to convert beta-carotene, most people don't convert beta-carotene very well."- Dr. Gabreil Cousens MD

It has been further shown that increasing beta-carotene in the diet reduces the conversion rate to vitamin A.[6] The human body can only convert very little beta-carotene to vitamin A, but nowhere near enough needed for daily human requirements. Individuals with thyroid problems or autoimmune disorders have even more difficulty with the conversion process. I have been a personal health coach for dozens of vegans with severe skin issues who refuse to acknowledge their issues are dietary. Vitamin A is paramount in reversing acne and other autoimmune disease by healing the intestinal lining. Those who do include the high Vitamin A foods I advise put their acne into remission and claim to have the best skin of their life thereafter.

B Complex Vitamins are the water-soluble vitamins. They play an innumerable number of roles in the body. They help to metabolize sugars, proteins and fats. They assist with liver function, ATP production, energy in the cell, brain functions, and more. The digestion and utilization of foods is greatly enhanced when consumed with B-complex vitamins. Most individuals who experience fatigue and metabolic dysfunction are low in B-complex vitamins. Due to them being water-soluble, a single traumatic event, stress, caffeine, alcohol and high sugar diets can cause rapid excretion of B-complex vitamins. They must be replenished often.

B1 Thiamine is involved in carbohydrate metabolism, energy production, oxygenation of the body, and normal nerve function. Food sources of B1 are liver, meats and eggs. Fruits and vegetables are very poor sources. Symptoms of low B1 include weight loss or weight gain, depression, fatigue, anxiety, constipation, retarded growth, nerve pain, and inflammation of the skin to just name a few.

---

[6] β-Carotene Conversion to Vitamin A Decreases As the Dietary Dose Increases in Humans. Janet A. Novotny, Dawn J. Harrison, Robert Pawlosky, Vincent P. Flanagan, Earl H. Harrison, and Anne C. Kurilich.

B2 Riboflavin is needed for energy production, fetal development, and proper mitochondria function. Food sources include organ meats, muscle meats and dairy products. Low B2 is associated with inflammation of the skin, cracks on sides of mouth and fatigue.

B3 Niacin is critical for brain function and energy production. B3 performs hundreds of chemical reactions in the body. Food sources include organ meats, muscle meats, brewers yeast and nutritional yeast. Low B3 symptoms include fatigue, weakness, retarded growth, low stomach acid, depression, mental problems, poor appetite, indigestion, skin diseases and more.

B5 Pantothenic Acid is crucial for the formation of adrenal hormones. The adrenal glands are amongst the most weak and compromised glands in modern people. They are severely degenerated in excessive coffee drinkers, vegans and vegetarians. The general populace does not fare much better either. Dark circles under the eyes and eye-bags are indicative of adrenal and kidney insufficiency, kidney stress, and adrenal exhaustion. Nutrient fortification with proper foods, diet and lifestyle, rejuvenate the kidney and adrenals to health. The eye-bags and dark circles disappear.

Food sources of B5 include liver, kidneys, brewers yeast, sourdough bread, soil grown wheatgrass juice and hearing. Fruits and vegetables are very poor sources. Low B5 is associated with weakness, GI disturbances, restlessness, fatigue, sleep disturbances and low resistance to stress and infections.

B6 Pyridoxine is needed for the synthesis of amino acids, proteins, hemoglobin, neurotransmitters, and regulation of blood sugar levels. It is needed for the proper metabolism of all foods, sugars, fats and proteins.

Food sources include liver, meats, nuts and seeds. Nuts and seeds contain B6 but it is incredibly difficult to obtain the amounts needed due to very high levels of anti-nutrients present in nuts and seeds. They are incredibly difficult to digest for children. Sunflower sprouts grown in a tray of soil can offer a plant source of B6. Deficiency includes skin issues, tissue break down, depression, fatigue, confusion and anemia.

Folic Acid is involved in amino acid metabolism, DNA synthesis, proper cell division, maturation of red blood cells, proper growth and development. Food sources include liver, kidney, muscle meats, and egg yolks have the highest amounts. It is one of the few vitamins found in high amounts in plant foods in plant foods as well. Plant sources are green vegetables, beans, legumes, mushrooms and yeast.

Biotin is needed for amino acid, carbohydrate and fatty acid metabolism. It is also required for new cell synthesis, for healthy hair, skin and nails. Egg yolk is the best food source of biotin followed by liver, kidney and whole grains prepared by proper fermentation, such as sourdough bread. Deficiency of biotin includes dandruff, skin disorders, hair loss, fatigue and lethargy.

B12 Methylcobalamin is one of the most important vitamins needed in the body. Most people cannot absorb B12 due to weak stomach acid production and loss of intrinsic factor. Deficiency is widespread in the population and worse amongst vegans and vegetarians. B12 is extremely important for myelin sheath formation, nerve health, blood formation and fat synthesis. Supplementing with B12 is crucial and most often individuals need to use intravenous methods of obtaining B12. Gluten, alcohol, and other plant toxins, can damage the stomachs ability to absorb B12. It is my belief that B12 deficiency is rampant in modern peoples, especially North Americans.

B12 is extremely heat sensitive and only found in raw animal products. Most modern people only receive it if they are breast fed as infants or consume raw dairy, or raw and rarely cooked meat. Food sources include raw kidney, liver, heart, beef, milk and egg yolk. There are no plant sources of B12. Deficiency of B12 includes nervous system disorders, memory loss, dementia, Alzheimers, weakness, fatigue, anemia, retarded development and much more.

Vitamin D is a fat-soluble vitamin that acts like a hormone in the body. It affects every bodily system. It enhances phosphorus and calcium absorption and utilization, proper mineralization of bones, immune health, cardiovascular health, and is cancer preventative. Fish or cod liver oil are best forms of supplementing with vitamin D.

There are also Vitamin D isolates available which are created by exposing cholesterol from sheep wool to UV radiation. This is the same process the human body and skin use to make vitamin D. Cholesterol in the blood reacts to sun light which penetrates the skin to form Vitamin D. Part of the reason for widespread vitamin D deficiencies in the population are due to low cholesterol, low-fat, genocidal, dietary recommendations. Vitamin D2 is a plant form and not usable by the body.

Food sources include fish liver oils, raw dairy and eggs. Deficiency of vitamin D include symptoms such as retarded or deformed bone growth, dental decay, bone weakness, heart disease, diabetes, depression, chronic fatigue, muscle wasting, hypertension, dementias and periodontal disease.

Vitamin F Essential Fatty Acids are composed of

essential fatty acids arachidonic, linoleic and linolenic acids. They are essential fatty acids needed for proper cellular membrane function and prostaglandin synthesis. They are abundant in wild fish, grass feed or pastured meats and dairies. Grain fed commercial livestock do not have the fatty acid profile needed to maintain health due to consuming unnatural diets. Commercial livestock are fed grain and not fresh pastures, which change the fatty acid composition of the meat.

Food sources include sardines, krill, wild salt-water fish, wild game, grass fed meets, grass fed or pastured dairy, and pastured eggs. Commercial animals, commercial dairy and farmed fish, are extremely poor sources. Plant sources are negligible. Symptoms of deficiency are dry skin, mental disorders, ADD, brain fog, retarded mentation, retarded brain development, impaired cell membrane permeability, resulting in impaired nutrient absorption and detoxification, hormonal imbalances, and inflammation.

Vitamin K2 is a fat-soluble vitamin found in pastured organ meats, eggs and butter. It was initially discovered by Dr. Price and was termed by him as "The X-factor". It is a primary nutrient which works in cohort with other minerals and vitamins to develop strong bones, large skulls, wide dental arches and help to prevent tooth decay. It was later discovered to also play a most prominent role in repairing arteries as well as clearing arteries of calcification. **It is needed along with Vitamin D to help bones properly absorb calcium and avoid calcification of arteries and organs. Without vitamin D and K2, calcium supplements calcify and harden the arteries.**

This is one of the reasons I warned against long term use of supplements. Long term used of isolated vitamin and mineral supplements has unforeseen consequences. It is well understood today, that the advise to supplement with calcium played an instrumental role in exasperating cardiovascular disease and calcification of arteries. The body does not utilize isolated nutrients very well. They are good for a short time only. Calcium without Vitamin K2 and D, flows into the body unregulated, and ends up in places it should not be, such as organs and arteries.

Food sources of K2 include pastured eggs, butter and organ meats. Vitamin K2 is found in nutrient-dense animal foods in conjunction with vitamins A, D and P, as well as all the minerals and coenzymes needed for proper absorption and utilization of these nutrients. These vitamins come in a package, when obtained from nature, in the form of whole-foods. The body recognizes them as food and incorporates these nutrients into its physiology seamlessly.

Deficiency of vitamin K2 results in dental decay, narrow faces and dental arches, shrinking brains, calcification of arteries, and brittle bones.

"[Activator X] plays an essential role in the maximum utilization of body-building minerals and tissue components; its presence can be demonstrated readily in the butterfat of milk of mammals, the eggs of fishes and the organs and fats of animals; it has been found in highest concentration in the milk of several species, varying with the nutrition of the animal; and it is synthesized by the mammary glands and plays an important role in infant growth and also in reproduction." - Dr. Price, *Nutrition and Physical Degeneration.* La Mesa, CA: Price-Pottenger Nutrition Foundation, 1939.

Heme Iron is a mineral critical for healthy blood and proper oxygenation of bodily tissues. It is important for proper hormonal function, brain development, and growth of muscle tissues. Developing children and menstruating women especially need proper iron.

Heme iron is found only in the blood, organs and muscles of animals. When heme iron is consumed in the diet by way of animal products, it comes with cofactors such as hemoglobin. Plant sources of iron are not heme iron. The body prefers the use of heme iron from flesh. Plant sources of iron are not heme iron because they do not contain cofactors such as hemoglobin found in animal meats. Plant sources contain an elemental form of iron that is not bioavailable due to anti-nutrients present in many plant foods. Heme iron from animal foods are thirteen times more bioavailable than the iron found in plant foods.

Symptoms of iron deficiency include anemia, extreme fatigue, weakness, pale skin, hair loss, shortness of breath, fast heartbeat and irregular menstruation. Women who are iron deficient tend to bleed more than usual when menstruating, or lose their period altogether. Anemia is extremely common in vegans and vegetarians. Women suffer considerably worse due to menstruation and constant loss of iron.

Amino Acids are critical for proper recovery and regeneration of bodily tissues, ATP production, development, and growth. It is a myth that by combining different plant seeds and legumes one can obtain complete proteins. Instead what should be considered are the full spectrum of amino acids, in bioavailable form.

Plants are utterly lacking in crucial amino acids needed for proper healing and regeneration. It is not that they do not contain amino acids. The problem is that they have very poor quality protein that are in bio-unavailable forms, that can not be relied upon for proper healing, growth and regeneration. Remember, grains, beans, legumes, and nuts are plant seeds which do not want to be eaten. They contain intrinsic defense chemicals designed to ward off predation. These defense mechanisms include protease inhibitors which block the absorption of amino acids, oxalates and tannins which block iron absorption, phytates which block zinc, calcium and magnesium absorption, amongst many other defense mechanisms. Chronic protein deficiency is a national endemic exasperated by the plant-based and vegan protein myth.

Oftentimes, victims of vegan diets may suffer from hair loss. It is due in most part to the lack of bioavailable protein in the diet, as well as the gut damage they endure as a consequence of their copious consumption of plant defense compounds, which damage the gut.

"The concept that all proteins are of comparable nutritional value is flawed and should be rejected by anyone interested in planning healthful diets."- Ottoboni, A., F. Ottoboni, 2013. *The Modern Nutritional diseases and How to Prevent Them*, 2nd Edition. Vincente Books, Fernley, NV.

Carnitine is a conditional essential amino acid made of lysine and methionine and is abundant in animal foods. It does not exist in plant foods. It is important for brain function and energy balance. Carnitine is found in muscle and organ meats. Deficiencies of carnitine result in fatigue, weakness, lethargy and brain fog.

Carnosine is an amino acids found primarily in the muscle tissue and organs of the body. It has many important functions in the body, the most important of which are anti-aging. Part of these anti-aging functions are anti-glycation. Glycation occurs when sugars are unnaturally bound to proteins, lipid molecules and cellular membranes in the body, as alluded to in the chapter on fruit-sugar. This process of glycation or fusing of sugar with protein and fats, causes oxidation, premature aging and free-radical damage.

Sugar also causes cross-linking of proteins which result in skin wrinkles and brain fiber degradation.

Carnosine helps to reverse the process. Vegans are in a constant state of glycation with virtually no carnosine in the diet. They are on diets which accelerate the aging process. Great sources of carnosine are organs and skeletal muscle of animals. Carnosine does not exist in plant sources.

Deficiencies of carnosine result in brain fog, wrinkled and shriveled skin, weakness, fatigue, poor circulation, and diabetes. Diabetics often have A1C levels tested in their bloodstream. This is a measure of sugar unnaturally linked to hemoglobin, which disrupts function, causes free radicals, oxidation, and organ damage in the body. Carnisone helps reverse the process and remove the sugar bound to hemoglobin, proteins and fats. Diabetes is essentially premature aging driven by a carbohydrate or sugar heavy diet. Vegans and vegetarians are especially prone to premature aging due to lack of carnosine and diets which rely entirely on carbohydrates or sugars.

Taurine is a sulfur containing amino acid important in the metabolization of fats. It is found primarily in animal tissues. It's functions pertain to maintaining proper hydration, forming bile salts, regulating minerals, regulating immune health, supporting eye and nervous system health.

Great sources of taurine are organ meats, skeletal muscle, and eggs. Taurine does not exist in plants. Deficiencies of taurine include digestive issues, low birth weights, weakening of muscles, retinal degeneration, hypothyroidism, kidney disorders, depression and anxiety. Those who do not consume meat or eggs lack the necessary enzymes needed to produce taurine.

Creatine is an amino acid most abundant in muscle tissue of humans and animals. Creatine is stored as phosphocreatine in muscle tissue, where it is used for energy. It is important for muscular endurance, mental endurance and brain function.

Sources of creatine are organ meats and muscle meats. Creatine does not exist in plants. Symptoms of creatine deficiency include fatigue, muscle weakness, lethargy, intellectual retardation, slow thinking, slow and slurred speech.

New vitamins and coenzymes are constantly discovered in animal foods which are thought to contribute to human development and well-being. Conversely, new plant-toxins are also constantly discovered, which only prove the unsuitability and digestibly of vegan diets for human beings. Certain vitamin and mineral interdependencies have been discovered but there are still far more which nutritional science has yet to discover.

Calcium supplements were advertised to the general public by financial interests until the general public realized calcium supplements without vitamins D and K2 were contributing to arterial calcification. Without the necessary co-vitamins, the body can not properly absorb and store calcium. Excess Vitamin A without Vitamin D, or vice verse, cause an imbalance between A and D ratios. It is important that individuals consume nutrient-dense foods in addition to proper supplementation. Additional examples of vitamin interdependency's are;

- Vitamin A with zinc
- B1 with manganese
- B6 and magnesium
- Choline with magnesium and calcium
- D with calcium

Animal foods contain most nutrients we need, in their proper form, and without any anti-nutrients which could inhibit nutrient absorption. Plant foods are missing a plethora of key nutrients needed for health and development, with little bioavailability of the meager amount they do contain. They can furnish only trace-minerals, electrolytes, and carbohydrates, which do play a role in a healthy, omnivorous diet.

By partaking in vegan and or plant-based diets, such as The Standard American diet, individuals actively starve themselves of fat-soluble vitamins, minerals, and amino acids, needed for optimal health and development. Today, youth are overwhelmed with an ocean of misinformation. Popular websites, so called nutritional experts, and industrial interest misguide and take advantage of unsuspecting youth. Lofty claims such as vegan diets providing all the building blocks, amino acids, and nutrients needed for human growth and development, are unfounded with no scientific basis.

CHAPTER 6

Analysis of Human, Carnivore & Herbivorous Digestive Systems

The formation and basis of all nutrients begin with minerals in the form of hard rock found in The Earth's soils. Plant life incorporate hard minerals into their structure with the assistance of symbiont soil-microorganisms, who are equipped with the metabolic machinery to digest and break down hard rocks. Soil microorganisms deliver hard minerals (rocks) to plant roots and in exchange receive plant sugars.

A single handful of healthy soil from an organic garden or forest floor, can contain up to fifty-billion microorganisms. These ecological systems do not exist in modern chemical agriculture as the synthetic additives, fertilizers and pesticides, kill biological life and render the soil lifeless. There is a symphony in healthy soil, whereby plants and an entire microcosmic universe of biological lifeforms, create interdependent and holistic ecosystems.

Human and animals do not have the ability to eat and digest hard rock. We understand this as do the animals, and leave this role to the bacteria and plants. It is the role of microorganisms in nature, to up-regulate nutrients in the form of hard rocks into the food chain and into the structure of plant bodies.

The next step in the ecological chain is fulfilled by herbivorous animals and ruminants. The digestive systems and eating habits of herbivorous animals differ to an extreme degree when compared to carnivores and human beings. Herbivorous animals graze on plant matter 12 or more hours a day, in order to fulfill nutritional requirements. They need to graze all day because vegetation is a nutrient-poor food.

Traditional cultures understood the limited ability humans have for digesting plant foods and for this very reason, developed fermented plant products. Foods such as sauerkraut, kimchi, pickles, and hundreds of other fermented vegetables, were produced by traditional cultures because they knew the fermentation process made them more digestible and assimilable by the human body. When plant foods are fermented, they are partially broken down by bacteria and do not pose as much of a threat to the human digestive tract.

Herbivorous animals have several stomachs equipped with cellulose digesting bacteria which help to break down plant matter, and convert it into saturated fat and protein. Humans are not equipped with the same type cellulose digesting bacteria. Though herbivores are on a high carbohydrate diet, they absorb it all as saturated fat and protein. In healthy human beings, the stomach has no bacteria like we find in herbivores. The human stomach is the most sterile part of the body. Beneficial bacteria do exist in the colon of human beings, but not the stomach. Bacteria in the stomach of human beings leads to illness's such as those which we find in vegans and high carbohydrate dieters.

You often hear of absurd claims and comparisons by so called vegan health authorities, who advocate for plant-based diets by pointing to the strength and size of ruminant animals such as bison, ox, bulls, cows or other herbivorous great apes such as chimpanzees, orangutans and gorillas.

These so called nutritional experts forget to mentions that all herbivores absorb plant matter as protein and fat.

They do not absorb them as carbohydrates the way humans do. Herbivorous animals absorb plant matter as if they were eating large amounts of animal protein and fat.

Human beings do not have the ability to convert carbohydrate foods into saturated fat and protein the way herbivores do. We absorb carbohydrate or plant foods as sugar. The strong, powerful animals, that the vegan zealots are alluding to, are on high fat, high protein diets, despite subsisting off of plants. We humans can only mimic such high protein and high fat diets by consuming animals because it is what our digestive system demands.

Digestive differences between herbivores and humans

The ruminant digestive system consists of 4 stomach compartments, with which they ferment food with the assistance of cellulose digesting bacteria. This fermentation process in their stomachs makes the plant nutrients bioavailable, and converts the plant matter from carbohydrate into saturated fat and protein. Most of the plant matter is actually converted into short chain fatty acids, which is similar to the animal fat we have been told to avoid in our own diets. In other words, these ruminants are on a high fat diet!

Zoologist have calculated that a cow chews a mouthful of grass two-hundred times before it sends it down to the rumen or stomach. In the stomach, bacteria ferment the cellulose and extract what they can and then send it back to mouth. The cow regurgitates it (vomits it into the mouth), chews it again another two-hundred times, before sending it back to the rumen (stomach), where bacteria continue to ferment on, or break down, the cellulose. This occurs dozens of times to extract the little nutrition available in the difficult to digest cellulose fiber. Further, it is with the aid of the bacteria and their fermentation process, that ruminant animals are able to neutralize many of the anti-nutrients and plant toxins inherent to plants.

The human being is not capable of fermenting cellulose in the stomach. The human stomach is designed to digest and metabolize proteins and fats from animals foods. Many illness's and diseases are caused by consuming carbohydrate foods, which end up putrefying and fermenting in the stomach and GI tract. This occurs when foods are not digested properly and instead the body must rely on yeast organisms such as candida, to convert sugars from carbohydrates or plants, into methane gas, alcohol, vinegar, acetaldehyde and many other toxic substances. These substances end up damaging the GI tract, internal organs, the brain and skin. The first and most common symptom of this fermentation process are symptoms of gas, bloating, dandruff, dandruff induced hair loss, psoriasis, and other fungal related skin issues. The symptoms cascade into worse illness's with time if the diet is not corrected.

Instead of bacteria, the human stomach relies on endogenously produced stomach acid and enzymes such as pepsin, trypsin, chymotrypsin, and lipase, amongst many others. These are powerful acidic enzymes, produced by the stomach and designed to break down only one group of foods, animal foods. That includes meat, fish, eggs and milk. They are not designed to or capable of, breaking down cellulose or fiber. Human digestive enzymes have absolutely no effect on cellulose or plant fibers. That is why we refer to plant foods as fiber, because they pass through the digestive tract without being digested and assimilated.

The enzymes produced by the human stomach break down animal flesh into amino acids and fatty acids. The stomach churns the food with these powerful enzymes and hydrochloric acid, before sending the food down to the small intestine, which is designed specifically, to absorb nutrients from proteins and fats.

The human GI tract, just like the ruminants, is meant to absorb food and nutrition in the forms of amino acids and fatty acids. When ruminant animals complete the fermentation process of cellulose in their stomach's, the fermented food passes down into the intestine as bioavailable fatty acids and amino acids, where they are absorbed by the intestinal lining as such. When humans consume plants, they are not broken down into amino acids and fatty acids. They pass into the digestive tract undigested, fermenting where they should not be, and cause damage to the gut lining, precipitating and exasperating autoimmune related disorders.

Herbivores and ruminants play a crucial role in their respective part of the food chain, converting carbohydrates or plant matter, into animal protein and fat. Humans and other obligatory carnivores fulfill the next role or link in the chain, by consuming the protein and fat directly from the herbivorous animal. There is a perfect, co-dependent, ecological, cycle of life, in which each creature uptakes nutrients and fulfills its role in the food chain, beginning with microorganisms and ending with carnivores.

Digestive differences between herbivorous great apes and humans

In order for mammals to obtain enough caloric energy and nutrition from food, they must consume either a very energy-dense diet, or be equipped with a very large gut, with which they can ferment and absorb food. The two apes most closely related to humans are chimps and gorillas, and have a genetic constitution which is about 98% identical. When we examine the physiology and digestive systems of these great apes, and compare them to human beings, we find that they are utterly different.

In the great apes, such as chimps and gorillas, we find that the hind-gut, or colon, compromises about 50% of the total gut mass. In humans the colon only compromised 10% of total gut mass. This hind-gut or colon, is the very end of the digestive tract. Animals with large hind-guts are classified as hind-gut fermenters, because unlike ruminants such as cows, who use multiple stomach chambers to ferment and digest plant matter, these great apes are equipped with large colons designed to break down plant matter. Plant matter is digested in the cecum and large intestine or colon of great apes, with the aid of symbiotic, cellulose digesting bacteria.

Contrast this with the human gut, where the colon only compromises 10% of the total gut mass, as opposed to 50% in gorillas and chimpanzees. Most of the human gut mass is composed of the upper or smaller intestine, which is not designed to ferment and digest plant matter. The human upper or smaller intestine, is a sterile environment designed to digest and absorb protein and fat, and is where the bulk of nutrient absorption occurs. The upper intestine compromises 70% of the total gut mass in human beings, and is the dominant digestive organ.

The colon of the great apes protrude through their belly's because of the large amount of plant fibers in their diets. These plant fibers are digested and broken down in the colon, not the stomach or upper intestines. The human gut only protrudes when indigestible fibers are consumed in the diet, causing bloating, gas and digestive discomfort, leading to all manners of disease. This is readily evident in the protruding stomachs of the great apes such as gorillas who are fit for high fiber diets.

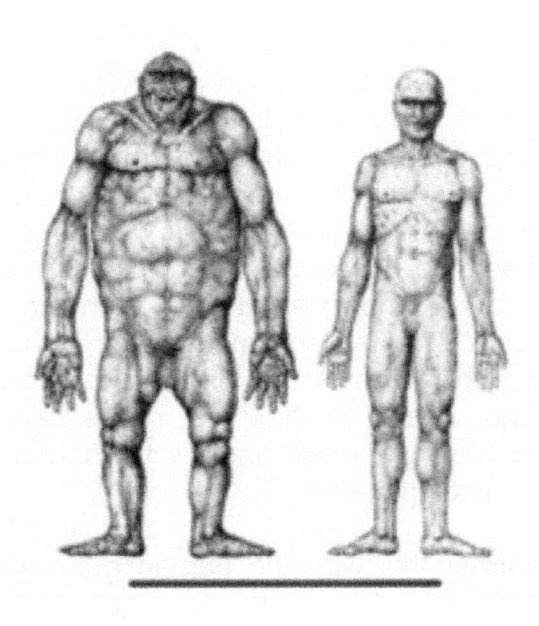

The large colons of hind-gut fermenters allow them to feed in bulk sizes and slowly graze all day. The symbiotic bacteria in their colons break down plant fibers, unlock nutrient value, and ferment the carbohydrates into fat and protein. The great apes are on a high fat and protein diet, just like cows and other carnivores. Though they consume carbohydrate vegetation, their digestive system absorbs it as if they were consuming flesh foods in the form of amino and fatty acids.

Oftentimes, the great apes will consume their own feces in order to better extract nutritional value from fiber. Consuming their feces, allows the apes to more easily extract nutritional content from fiber, which has been predigested by the bacterial colonies of their colons. Next time a vegan asks you to eat like a gorilla, insist that they consume their own feces as well, to demonstrate that the gorilla diet is suitable for human beings.

It is estimated that the microbial fermentation of fibers in the colons of great apes supply up to 75% of their energy requirements. Contrast this with humans who can at most extract only 2 to 8% of their energy requirement from the colon. The colon is of such great significance to the great apes that they will die if it is amputated. Conversely human beings have little to no problem when needing to amputate the colon, as it is the least significant organ in regards to the digestion and absorption of nutrition. This is evident in patients who have undergone colonectomies.

If we examine the gut proportions of the great apes, we find that again, the human being is utterly different. The small or upper intestine, plays the most prominent role in our gut composition resembling other carnivores. The upper intestines only absorb nutrients from animal foods. The upper intestines release hydrochloric acid and receive bile from the gallbladder. Bile and hydrochloric acid are only capable of breaking down animal protein and fat, not plant matter.

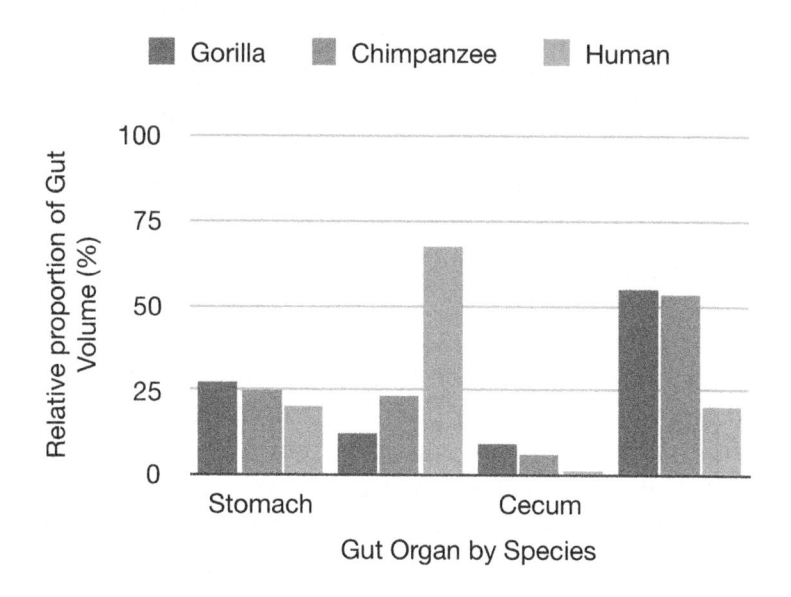

In total, you have stomach acid, a plethora of enzymes and bile, all produced by the human body, which are catered, designed and suitable, only for the digestion of animal foods. It is plainly obvious that humans are meant to eat animal foods. These enzymatic secretions, acids, and biles, are specific for animal protein and fat digestion. These enzymes and acids do not digest cellulose.

The cecum and colon which are used by hind-gut fermenters to digest cellulose, are relatively small in human beings. It is not humanly possible to live on or sustain off of plants without running into problems. Vegan dietitians and nutritionist will insist that eating only salads with proper supplementation constitutes a healthy diet. They have no sense of higher human development and potential.

The human digestive system does not have the ability to extract nutrients from plant fibers. The plant world is very much indigestible for humans and passes through the entire digestive tract, where it ends up in the colon undigested. It is in the colon that humans can make some use of plant fiber. In the human colon, bacteria break down and convert some cellulose into fatty acids. Prior to the colon, plant matter travels through 15 feet of small intestine, where it provides absolutely no nutritional value. Instead, it causes gas, bloating, indigestion, and inhibition of nutrient absorption. It damages the gut-lining and causes systemic inflammation, which include damage and stress to organs, glands and nerves.

The plant-based and vegan pundits, the so called vegan health authorities, and the financial establishment, do not wish to acknowledge or understand the laws of nature. They do not care to study the natural world objectively, nor do they genuinely care for the health of fellow human beings or the planet. The plant-based public relations campaign and vegan agenda, does not even have to do with the welfare of animals. The public has fallen prey to vegan zealots who have masqueraded their cult under the guise of nutritional science.

Until recently, these zealots existed on the fringes of society, where the collective subconscious instinctively understood that they were amongst the most weak and least healthy in society. Due to the new sustainable development goals which have become the most dominant forces in commerce, politics and industry as of late, powerful financial interest have thrown their weight behind the vegan agenda. A well funded, very well organized, vegan public relations campaign has been inoculated into Western Society, through the use of documentaries, films and celebrity culture. This agenda has no consideration for the truth, the science and the facts, in regards to human health.

CHAPTER 7

Anthropological Records & Human Desire of Animal Fat

Throughout human history, humans have sought after and glorified the fat of animals for healing, sustenance, nourishment and energy. This fact is not only recorded in anthropological and ethnographical studies, but also in folklore and mythology all over the world. Nutrient-dense animal fats were revered as holy foods. Indigenous peoples and cultures always understood them as playing the primary role in proper growth, development, fertility, and life sustenance.

No matter the culture you look at around the world, people used whatever animal fats were available to them in their surroundings, and highly prized them. In Dr. Price's work, he recorded how the Swiss people of the Loetschental Valley used butter for candles in church. The act was symbolic of their appreciation to deity for the butter which they understood as playing a key role in the healthy development and sustenance of their people. Dr. Price's monumental ethnographical work, *Nutrition and Physical Degeneration,* documents countless peoples and tribes who venerated their local fat sources. The book is a testament that will stand the test of time against the pseudo-scientific nutritional literature and ideas circulating in the mainstream today.

A very interesting excerpt comes from a book written by Henno Martin and his experience with fellow geologist

Herman Korn. They were German geologist serving the Nazi regime in Germany during the 2nd world war. After the 2nd world war, both had decided that they did not want to be imprisoned for war crimes and instead took refuge in the Namimbia Desert of Africa, where they lived amongst primitive bushmen. Neither wanted any part in the war which they strongly opposed. They decided to live off the land until the war ended. The following is an excerpt from Henno Martin's Book, *The Sheltering Desert,* in which he recorded their experiences.

"It was a big day for us when we bagged the first fat zebra, for we had an indescribable longing for fat, and now the grazing was becoming more lush, the game was getting plump. During our own shortage of fat, we were reminded of the Bushmen's idea of heaven. When a bushman dies he wanders over a stony waste until he comes to the heavenly Kraal, which is fenced in by thorn bushes. At the entrance hangs gourd full of warm fat, and next to it a scoop. Before he enters heaven, the bushman may drink as much fat as he likes. Such is heaven to the Bushmen, for he lives on the edge of the wilderness and usually in great hardship. When we first heard this legend it struck as a mere curiosity. Now that we had some personal experience of life in the desert we could see the point. For two days our big iron pot was on the embers full of juicy rib pieces , and whenever we felt like it, we finished out generous tit-bits and drank spoonfuls of the warm fatty liquid"- Henno Martin, *The Sheltering Desert*, pg. 217

Another interesting excerpt comes from a book written in 1920, *The Friendly Arctic- The Story of 5 Years in The Polar Region,* by Vilhjaimur Stefansson.

"There was a time when fat was a much more important element than it is now in the diet of the European. That was before the time of sugar. Four-hundred years ago ordinary sugar was unknown in Europe and the amount eaten in the form of honey or sweet fruits was negligible when compared with the present-day huge consumption. Three-hundred years ago, sugar was the luxury of kings, and two-hundred years ago it was a rarity in the diet of ordinary man. Even within our own time, the per-capita income has increased enormously. And this article of food which some people imagine to be a prime necessity, and which others even think to be essential to health, is really a newcomer in the diet even to us. But as sugar has increased in favor, fat has lost taste. The relationship between the two has always been reciprocal-the more sugar, the less fat."

That was written one-hundred years ago by Viljaimur Stfansson, and it is true even today but to a more extreme degree. Official government and medical dietary guidelines, as well as vegan propagandist, have been encouraging Americans to cut out animal fat from their diets in favor of carbohydrates or sugar for one-hundred years now. I will elaborate how that happened and why in later chapters. It is totally baseless, not founded on science but on financial interests. Pharmaceutical and the mega-agricultural food industries have profited immensely at the demise of the public's health.

Nutrient and energy-dense fats always have been the most critical component in our diet, evolution and development. Without these fats, we would have not been human. We would have not developed larger brains and the higher thinking that distinguishes us from all the other great apes. The anthropological evidence shows that fat played the most important role in our diets. Every human culture prior to industrial civilization, relished and sought after animal fat. Below is a list of several indigenous tribes and the fat sources which they relished. This is by no means a comprehensive list.

- The Indo-Iranian and Turkic nomads of Central Asia's steppe subsisted off of sheep fat.
- The indigenous Canadian tribes relished and lived off of mouse fat.
- Berbers and Arabs of North Africa and The Middle East relished camel fat.
- The Lapsemian Siberians relished reindeer fat.
- The Native Americans of the Plains and Continental North relished pemmican.
- Coastal Salish Tribes relished ooligan grease which is a fat derived from fish.
- The Inuit ate walrus, whale and seal fat.
- The Australian Aborigines sought after emu fat.
- The Maasai people of Kenya and Tanzania sought after fat and milk of cattle.
- Coastal oriental peoples relished all and any fat sources they could obtain from the sea and land.

John Speeth, a well respected zoo-archeologist wrote, **"Fat, not protein, seemed to play a very prominent role in the hunters decisions about what animals to kill and which body parts to discard or take away."**- John D. Speth, *The Paleoanthropology and Archeology of Big Game Hunting.*

Jack Brink, a well respected archaeologist and curator at The Royal Alberta Museum in Edmonton, Canada writes in his book, **"Fat, not meat, was the food source most sought after by all plains aboriginal hunting cultures."**- Jack Brink, *Imagining Heads Smashed In.*

Please do not confuse plant fat for animal fat. Ancient man specifically hunted and sought after animal fat. Only animal fat has the fat-soluble vitamins and minerals crucial for human development. Only animal fat can be used as a fuel source within the human body, not plant fat. Plant fats and oils solidify in the human body due to their incompatibility with human physiology. Furthermore, plant fat, or vegetable oils, were non-existent in the natural world until the advent of human hybridization of plants and industrial oil processing.

For some reason, dietary anthropology and nutritional ethnography seems to be completely ignored by state sponsored nutritional curriculums, as well as vegan and plant-based diet pundits. According to the works of nutritional pioneers such as Dr. Price, mental and physical illness were completely unknown by the primitive and isolated cultures. We do not even have to look at historical records to grok the fact that man was an animal fat hunter and designed to consume animal fat. In contrast, our modern, disease ridden culture, excludes or severely limits almost all animal-fat sources from the diet. This is totally unprecedented in the history and evolution of man.

Many cultures still exist around the world today who subsist off of natural diets which relish and value animal fat as the most important part of the diet. These isolated cultures suffer no heart disease and are often called "centenarian cultures", due to the high prevalence of individuals who live to one-hundred years of age. These cultures can be found in Pakistan amongst the Hunza, in Afghanistan amongst all the rural Pashtuns, Tajiks, Uzbeks and Hazaras, in Japan amongst The Okinawans, in The Caucasus amongst the Circassians, Abkhaz and Kabardians amongst many more.

In recent times, vegan and plant-based pundits have attempted to use these cultures to promote their own agenda's, encouraging plant-based diets. They have misconstrued the cultures and have made it seem as if they are vegans or subsist wholly of plants. The fact of the matter is that these people relish the animals fats. In rural Afghanistan the tribes relish diary and sheep fat, the Okinawans relish pork fat, the Hunza of Pakistan and the tribes of the Caucuses relish dairy and cattle fat, and also credit milk kefir for their longevity and robust health.

This is not to say that they only consume fat either. **These people place the greatest value on the animal fats in their diet,** but they also obtain vegetation, nuts, seeds, tubers, starches, and fruits from their environment. They all have varying levels of macro-nutrient compositions. None of them are eating for health. All of them are eating to survive by simply choosing what the land gives them abundantly and in season. By obeying natural law in their own environment, they live healthy, long lives, without disease or illness. The key here is, the emphasis on animal fats as the most critical component of the diet.

Humans have a natural desire to seek out and consume animal fat, not plant matter. It is programmed into us by nature because it is what we were designed to eat. Although I had intellectually come to understand this fact, it was my first hand experience with consuming animal fat after long stints on vegan diets, that radically changed my perception on diet and nutrition. A personal story I would like to share is my experience consuming meat after abstaining from meat consumption for 6 months.

In the summer of 2016, I had the good fortune of reuniting with a good friend of mine. I had known him from our ancestral lands in Afghanistan. When we met again in California after 5 years, he was shocked when he witnessed my physical degeneration and the rapid aging process I experienced. I was always know as a handsome and well built lad amongst my peers and community, until I started to experiment with vegan diets.

He asked me if I was on drugs and I responded to him that I was experimenting with vegan diets. He laughed at me with hysteria and stated that I looked like a junkie. I was breaking out in acne and my face gave off a shriveled and aged appearance. I was also dealing with insomnia, hair loss, brain fog and fatigue. Throughout my several years stint with veganism, I would occasionally "cheat", and consume creamy ice creams. I did not understand that my body was instinctively craving animal fat.

My friend insisted that I allow him to cook me a meat meal. After several hours of his persistence, I gave in and allowed him to cook for us. He had decided to cook ox-tail meat in a broth. Ox-tail is the most collagenous and most fatty piece of tissue on a male bull. Upon my first bite of the ox-tail, I felt an immediate rush of endorphins run into my body. The sensations grew stronger and stronger, until I felt what I could only describe as "a gapping hole healing in my brain". I literally felt my brain absorbing and integrating the animal fat. It was at that moment that I had realized just how starved I had been of true nutrition. My experience reminds me of Henno Martin's experience with animal fat when he was hiding out in the harsh desert.

In Central Asia and isolated valleys of Afghanistan, centenarian cultures are also very dominant. The collective instinct of the people understands that a diet without animal fat is a famine diet. It does not matter how much carbohydrates are available, if animal fat and protein are not supplied in the diet, it is generally recognized as form of starvation.

There exist in Central Asia and Afghanistan a popular form of sport called buzkashi, which translates as "goat pulling". It is a rough and dangerous sport, where horse-mounted contestants attempt to place a goat carcass in a goal, similar to soccer. The difference here is that players are mounted on horses and the competition is typically very fierce, leading to severe injuries when riders are thrown off of horses. Due to the dangerous and physically demanding nature of the sport, buzkashi players consume diets slightly different than the rest of the population. Instead of consuming just any cut of meat, they consume the fattiest cuts of meats and organs, in order to rapidly repair and regenerate bodily tissue.

The players also prefer to have additional skeletal muscle, larger frame size, greater bone mass density, and thicker subcutaneous fat, in order to develop more strength and resilience for their sport. The cuts of meats in their diets include ox-tail, eyeballs, brain, liver, kidney, tongue and heart.

It was due to this instinctual knowledge, that my friend had fed me ox-tail when I reunited with him in California. He understood that I needed animal fat because of his familiarity with indigenous dietary principles from Afghanistan. He instinctively understood that the integrity of my body was coming apart due to over consumption of plant-foods. The plant foods literally rip apart the gut-lining and destroy the collagen of the body. He fed me the most cholesterol and collagenous rich meat he could find. My inflammation and symptoms came to a near halt overnight.

It is important to note that in the wild, lions and other carnivorous predators, eat the organs, fat and marrow of their prey first. They typically leave the lean meat for scavengers such as jackals, hyenas and vultures.

In later years, I again experimented in ox-tail consumption with my wife. Ox-tail is very different from the cuts of meats which are available in western grocery stores. The experiment was undergone to see if we would notice any changes in our health. We cooked ox-tail in a pressure cooker with several herbs and water. We consumed both the soup and the meat. It was a great tasting dish.

My wife ended up feeling severe nausea after we ate, due to the overwhelming amount of fat in the dish. Our Western appetites and pallets are not trained to consume such foods as we have subsisted off of unnatural amounts of sugar for generations now. Ironically enough, the next morning upon awakening, she realized that all of her wisdom teeth which for years were only slightly visible and covered by gum tissue, had grown in completely. A single high dose of proper fat-soluble vitamins, animal fat, and cholesterol, was able to further enlarge her skull capacity, which made room for her wisdom teeth to grow in over night.

I should emphasize here that individuals who read this book should not go rushing to extreme dietary changes and start consuming lots of animal fat. Most of the bodies in the Western World have lost the ability to digest fat and need retraining due to years of carbohydrate dominance in the diet. Do not confuse fatty meat with lean meat either. They are totally different. Instead, individuals should slowly add cuts of fatty meats and dairy products such as butter into the diet. Overtime, as the body begins to recognize and learn how to work with fat again, it will give you signals that it is ready for more fat in the diet.

Recall what I had written about Dr. Price's work. **All the indigenous cultures he studied had no dental decay, deformities or crowding. The wisdom teeth are meant to grow in normally, in a properly nourished and developed individual.** The extraction of wisdom teeth is prevalent in The West and other industrialized nations due to the ill-founded, fat-soluble vitamin, nutritional deprivation of the public. The skulls, dental arches, and mouths, do not fully mature and develop. This has far reaching consequences beyond just the cosmetics of the teeth. Parts of the brain atrophy and do not get a chance to develop.

It is only in the Modern West and in industrialized cities around the world, where man has been removed from his natural diet and environment. Industrialized peoples must come to relearn and form their own dietary principles. This abandonment of the natural world also renders them as prey to financial interests, who prefer a sick population that can be capitalized on. It is for the very reason of financial gain that the food-pyramids of the industrialized western nations advocate for low or no animal fat in the diet.

Individuals and families are also subject to a barrage of misinformation by vegan zealots, who masquerade their cult under the guise of health and nutrition. **The fact of the matter is, healthy diets vary widely, but the common substrate which unites them all is animal fat.** There have been cases of cultures who consume no carbohydrates and consume only animal foods, such as the Maasai and Inuit, but the opposite end of the spectrum does not exist. There are no cultures who consume only plant foods and no animal fat. There are cultures who consume large amounts of carbohydrates but in addition to animal fat. No instinctually aware culture would do such a thing excluding all animal fat. When I speak of culture here, I am specifically referring to pre-industrialized and isolated cultures. I am not referring to cultures that have been victim and subject to the foods and brainwashing of modern industry.

Some significant facts to point out in regards to the importance of animal fats and human dietary needs are, the fact that a mother's breast milk is composed of 54% saturated fat. Babies are on high saturated fat diets, in addition to the carbohydrate content of the milk. The saturated fats are needed to properly develop the babies organs, glands, nerves, eyes and most importantly, the brain. Vegan mothers who claim to nurse vegan children do not seem to understand that the child is on a high animal fat diet via her breast milk.

The needs for saturated fat and cholesterol is of such high significance in the diet, that the body will even use dietary carbohydrates and convert them to saturated fat in the liver. The problem with relying solely on carbohydrates for conversion to saturated fat, is that they do not come with fat-soluble vitamins that build the body. Excessive consumption of carbohydrates without animal fat also causes inflammation, and over time, cause fatty liver disease. The body uses all the food consumed to create cholesterol and saturated fat. The importance of this can not be emphasized enough. Everything the body does is to survive.

CHAPTER 8

Saturated Animal Fat & Cholesterol are The Most Anti-aging, Brain-building, & Health-Enhancing Nutrients Available to Humans

There are many so called "health experts" and nutritionist today, who have received sub-par educations due to the corporate oligarchs and their powerful lobbyist in Washington. One of the greatest myths which has been ingrained into the minds of physicians and nutritionist, and peddled onto the public, is that of saturated fat and cholesterol causing heart disease. They insist that the traditional wisdom of humanities ancestry is flawed, and that we have reached a new era of health with seed oils, refined carbohydrates, fad diets such as veganism, and medications. They really want you to believe that the food humans consumed for 99% of our existence is the cause of heart disease. This is a cruel joke.

The reality is that saturated fat and cholesterol, are the most crucial dietary components to robust physical and mental health, graceful aging, and longevity. It has been repeatedly proven in studies that higher cholesterol is correlated with longer lifespans. The entire body and brain function better with higher cholesterol. Every cell membrane is made of cholesterol, every neurotransmitter, every hormone.

The body needs cholesterol as raw material for all of its functions. It just so happens that in nature, the foods with the highest source of cholesterol, are only found in the most nutrient-dense animal foods, such as eggs, butter, and organ meats. Additionally, they are completely compatible with human physiology and digestion. The fact that we are meant to consume these foods is plainly obvious.

Peoples, nations and cultures, with the highest saturated fat intake, have the lowest rates of heart attacks. The French have notoriously low rates of heart attacks. Their diets consists of lots of saturated fat in the form of butter and cheese. Due to the sheer ignorance prevalent in nutritional circles, the consensus is that their low rates of heart attacks are due to their wine consumption, but actually, it is because they are eating what their body is made of, saturated fat and cholesterol.

The body is like a well oiled machine. Saturated fat and cholesterol are the fuel, oil, lubricant, moisturizer, healer and builder of the body. Nothing the body does is to kill itself. Cholesterol is so important for the body's health, that it will even convert the inflammatory carbohydrates in the diet into cholesterol.

The role that saturated fat plays in the body is more significant than any other dietary nutrient. Fat and cholesterol nourish every gland and organ, that includes the adrenals, the testes or ovaries, the intestines, the heart, thyroid and brain. It is needed in the production of all sex hormones and neurotransmitters, tissue production and healthy cell turnover. It creates healthy cell membranes, encouraging the proper absorption of nutrients, and detoxification of free radicals, environmental pollutants, heavy metals etc.

Cholesterol and saturated fat boost the immune system. This is due to the fact that all immune cells are formed from cholesterol. The immune cells of the body are primarily generated from the stem cells in the bone marrow, the very core of a human being. The bone marrow is a high fat, cholesterol rich organ. The bone marrow is replenished only by dietary saturated fat, cholesterol, and the nutrients found in them. High sugar or vegan diets, starve the bone marrow and rapidly accelerate the aging process.

Individuals on low animal fat diets and with low cholesterol have a hard time fighting infections and supporting the immune system. A body deficient in cholesterol is in starvation. What little cholesterol that is produced in the body by carbohydrate consumption, is distributed amongst all the starving organs of the body, and the immune system. I will reiterate again here, cholesterol is so important in the body, that it will use anything it can to get it. Even the plants consumed by vegans will be converted into cholesterol by the body, albeit with all of the oxidative and inflammatory side effects that come with plant foods and none of the vitamins and minerals that come with animal foods.

Saturated fat and cholesterol are also the best skin food. The skin needs and prefers animals fat for its cellular membrane. It is the food humans have evolved on for 99% of our evolution. The prevalence of dry, wrinkly, and acne prone skin in North America's youth, is due to saturated fat and cholesterol deficiencies. Saturated fat lubricates the skin, increases moisture and decreases dryness. If you look at cafeterias across North America's schools, there is not a gram of saturated fat and cholesterol available. The cafeterias are filled with refined carbohydrates, junk food, sugars and lean, processed meats.

Due to ATP and cellular preference for saturated fat as fuel, it also increases our energy, vitality, endurance, and any feelings of fatigue. Because it is the natural fuel meant for man, it does not come with the sugar highs and lows associated with carbohydrate consumption.

Fats from all sources, wether meat fats, dairy fats, or high quality monounsaturated oils, such as avocado oil or olive oil, have the ability to protect cells, organs and glands from environmental pollutants. At current time, our environments are unlike they have ever been in the history of the world. The industrialization process has released untold number of chemicals and pollutants into the air and water which are harmful to biological life.

The body will use fats to help buffer and remove pollutants from itself. In order for an environmental pollutant to be neutralized by the body, it must be stored in a fat molecule. If dietary fat is not available in the diet, then the body will need to store the environmental pollutants into bodily fat tissues. In leaner individuals, the need for dietary fat is even more paramount, as the body will have no choice but to store it in the fatty issue of the internal organs, such as the brain. A low-fat diet in the modern world, is the absolute worse thing one can conceive of. It is evil.

Take for example a study published by the Environmental Working Group. In research at two different laboratories, they found that the umbilical cords from 10 different babies born in American hospitals had on average 200 industrial pollutants and chemicals. Their tests revealed a combined 287 chemicals present in the group of babies. The umbilical cords of the babies contained pesticides, consumer product ingredients, garbage, gasoline and waste from burning coal, which includes mercury and other heavy metals. Of the 287 chemicals detected, it was concluded that 180 cause cancer, 217 were toxic to the brain and nervous system, and 208 caused birth defects or abnormal development. Humans have never been exposed to such an environment in the whole of their history. [7]

---

[7] A benchmark investigation of industrial chemicals, pollutants and pesticides in umbilical cord blood. Environmental Working Group, July 14, 2005. https://www.ewg.org/research/body-burden-pollution-newborns.

It is important to understand, that unless you are living in some isolated or remote part of the world, that you are also subject to exposer to all of these chemicals. They are in the food we eat, the water we drink, the air we breathe, the cosmetics we use, our very clothing, our cookware, perfumes and much more. We are living in a cesspool of carcinogenic and cancer causing toxins. There is no other food substance which better protects and buffers the body from these environmental toxins than fats. Several tablespoons of high quality, mono-seed oils are ok, but one can not consume them in the same quantity as they would with high quality animal fats, such as butter, creams or meats. Excess seed or vegetable oils, no matter how high quality they are, will clog the arteries and harden in the body. Individuals who are interested in learning more about the detoxification process of these industrial contaminants can read my book *Nutrition and Hair Loss; A New Perspective.*

When the body runs off of sugars or carbohydrates for fuels, it exhausts all the organs and degrades cells. Historically, humans only burnt sugar for fuel in times of famine or extremely stressful situations. The constant use of sugar or carbohydrates for fuel is a leading contributor to arterial inflammation.[8] The body responds to arterial inflammation by sending cholesterol to the site in order to quell inflammation, and repair arterial damage caused by sugars, plant toxins, environmental pollutants, and vegetable oils.

Cholesterol is a waxy like, healing substance inside the body. Overtime, high carbohydrate diets such as vegan or Standard American diets, continuously damage arteries

---

[8] Death by Carbs: Added Sugars and Refined Carbohydrates Cause Diabetes and Cardiovascular Disease in Asian Indians.
Bhaskar Bhardwaj, MD Evan L. O'Keefe, MS James H. O'Keefe, MD. pubmed:30228507.

and this leads to heart attacks. Yes, there is cholesterol present in the arteries of heart attack patients, but it is foolish to blame the heart attack on cholesterol. Cholesterol is just the repair substance. When the body suffers from a wound on the skin, the body also uses cholesterol to heal and repair the skin. Cholesterol is used in each and every single repair process in the body. It is no different in the arteries.

The side effects of diets low in cholesterol and high in carbohydrates as advocated by the US Food and Drug Administration, as well as vegan pundits, are powerful contributors to nearly all of our dietary related illness's. We cannot say that diet alone is the cause of disease and illness. Environment and psychology also play a prominent role. But no doubt that the high carbohydrate, low-fat, dietary advice, percolated onto the public over the last century, will be remembered as one of the most inhumane and cruel science experiments ever to be conducted on a nation. It is extremely deleterious for young, developing children.

Low dietary and blood cholesterol levels are associated with:

- Increased risk of heart disease.
- Increased risk of cancer.
- Associated with violence and suicide.
- Associated with Parkinson.
- Memory loss.
- Autoimmune diseases and poor immunity.
- Early death.
- Learning disabilities.

The brains composition is made of 60-70% fat. 40% of the brains fat is made of cholesterol. The myelin sheath which covers and protect sensitive nerves is made of 60% cholesterol. The brain, just like the rest of the body, has constant cellular turn over. Without adequate cholesterol, the brain does not have adequate building materials to self regenerate itself, protect itself, and perform it's vital functions. This causes many type of neuroses, mental illness and psychological disorders, especially in vegans who are utterly lacking and starving of cholesterol.

Carl Pfeiffer was a renowned American doctor who performed research on American prisoners. He discovered that more than 85% of violent offenders had low blood cholesterol.
Brains starved of saturated fat and cholesterol can not function properly. They become manic, angry, neurotic, depressed, easily irritated, and form aggressive personalities. These traits are very evident in the unfortunate youth and adults who are misled into so called "healthy" dietary regimens such as veganism. They express a type of manic activity, a religious zeal and fervor, for their vegan diets. These youth deserve our sympathy and are in need of help. A starving brain can not help itself.

In order to form memory, the brain needs synapses to function. Synapses are made entirely out of cholesterol and saturated animal fat. Brains starving of cholesterol and saturated fat can not form synapses, causing poor brain function, slow thinking and inability to remember things.

Mothers breast milk is very rich in cholesterol. Breast milk has an enzyme which insures that the baby digests and absorbs every particle of cholesterol. The brain, eyes, bone marrow and other fatty organs are made of cholesterol. The unfortunate prevalence of baby formula even amongst mothers who could afford to nurse their own babies, is one of the greatest offenses and crimes to the healthy development of a child. Most of these children unfortunately are no better off as they wean off of formula and onto low-fat diets. Very many people in the industrialized areas of the world have now for generations not been able to achieve proper brain development and psychological maturation, due to the intentional deprivation of saturated fats and cholesterol. The proper growth of the brain could never occur without proper animal fats.

In order for the brain and body to function properly, certain raw substances need to be available. No amount of plant matter can substitute for animal protein and fat, this is nature's mandate. Replenishing and fortifying the human body with the required animal nutrients, results in proper biochemical, hormonal, and neurotransmitter health. We are able to perceive the world more optimally when obeying natural law. If the brain and body are starved of certain nutrients, they will affect the mind and it's perception.

Dietary regimens devoid of animal fat and protein, are subject to excessive consumption of sugars or carbohydrates, creating blood sugar problems. Blood sugar problems are pivotal to mental and physical health. Blood sugar spikes from high carbohydrate meals causes an over arousal of the brain in the same way drugs do. The same parts of the brain which are aroused by drug use, are aroused by carbohydrates and blood sugar spikes. Further again, the blood sugar in the blood stream auto-oxidizes and creates free radical damage, accelerating the aging process and stressing organs. Sugars also demineralize the body of minerals and B-complex vitamins. These are all needed for a calm, healthy nervous system.

Blood sugar spikes from high carb or vegan diets also cause glycation of the brain which is the primary contributor to brain cell degeneration, alzeimers, Parkinson's and other degenerative diseases. Beta-amyloid proteins are glycated tangles of proteins that stick together in the brain and cause Alzeimers. The same damage that occurs in the brains of alcoholics is occurring in the brains of vegans, those on the standard American diet, or those on a high sugar diet. Only animal proteins and fats can help to regenerate brain cells. Only nutrients found in high concentrations and bioavailable forms, can feed the human nervous system. Anxiety and psychological disorders are an epidemic in North America and are driven primarily by leaky gut, food sensitivity, sugar, plant toxins, and nutrient deficiencies.

Renowned board-certified nutritionist, neuro-feedback specialist, and international best selling author, says of the effects of vegan diets on mental health, **"I can tell you from my own experiences as a clinician, and I am not alone amongst my colleagues, that by far the most damaged, intractably damaged brains and nervous systems I have ever encountered, have to the letter been vegetarians and especially vegans. These brains and nervous systems sometimes are so severely neurologically damaged that a good deal of it may even be irreversible."**- Nora Gedgaudes, CNS and author of *Primal body and primal mind: Beyond the paleo diet for total health and a longer life.* [9]

Depression is a mental illness which currently affects 66% of the population. The lack of cholesterol and fat-soluble vitamins in the diet inhibit the body and brains ability to produce hormones such as serotonin. Cholesterol and saturated fat are the primary building blocks for all of our hormones and this includes serotonin, dopamine, estrogen, testosterone, and progesterone. Natural laws must be obeyed if we are to experience feelings of well-being and happiness. These natural laws entail eating a diet mandated by nature and not one mandated by diet fanatics or the corporate-oligarchy.

The vegan, plant-based and Standard American diets, are a constant onslaught of brain damaging sugars

---

[9] Youtube/ Primal mind: Nutrition and Mental health by Nora Gedgaudes. Uploaded to Youtube by Nora Gedgaudes, 04/07/2013.

and carbohydrates. Vegan and Standard American diets shift the biochemistry of the body into a state of advanced aging and degradation. The body gets no chance or break. In these diets, the body is never fed the food that it needs. They are devoid of saturated fat, animal protein and cholesterol. It is a famine diet.

CHAPTER 9

Metabolism, Carbohydrates, Energy & Obesity

To further build the case for the absolute necessity of animal foods in the human diet, and the absurdity of veganism, we have to examine the metabolic differences between carbohydrate and fat metabolism. Although I have already noted the many shortcomings of vegan diets, such as their utter lack of nutrition, plant toxins, and sugar's effects on aging and disease, this book would not be complete without belaboring on the array of health benefits associated with burning fat for fuel.

Termed ketosis, it is a state where the body relies on, and burns fat molecules in the form of ketones for fuel. Babies are always in a state of ketosis and most everyone can reach ketosis in a fasted state or after 8 to 12 hours of sleep. The consumption of sugars, or plant carbohydrates around the clock inhibit the human body from achieving this metabolically advantageous state, where instead of burning sugar for fuel, we burn ketones.

Ketones are the most optimal energy unit for the brain and all other bodily systems. They are in fact the primordial fuel for the brain and body. Ketones are released or used by the body after blood sugar levels are cleared from the system. The smallest amounts of carbohydrate consumption will raise blood-sugar and insulin levels. When insulin or sugar is present in the blood stream, ketones can not be used by the body for fuel.

Most industrialized people and especially North Americans, have adapted to a very volatile and damaging source of fuel, sugar. Westerners have adapted to sugar metabolism, which ages them prematurely and contributes heavily to disease processes. In contrast, a low-sugar or low-carb diet, results in lower insulin levels, and greater ability to achieve a ketogenic state.

"If there is one single known marker for long life that is found in the centenarian and animal studies, it is low insulin levels."- Dr. Ron Rosedale M.D.

Diets which include some amount of animal fats, and that are not overly reliant on carbohydrates, allow the body to dig into, and use its own fat stores for energy. These fat stores are converted into ketones for energy usage. When we constantly consume carbohydrates throughout the day, such as in vegan diets, we inhibit the ability for the mitochondria or energy producers of our fat cell's, to use oxygen and respirate. We literally handicap our fat tissues. This results in energy reduction, fatigue, insulin resistance and inability to lose weight for those who are overweight or obese.

High carb diets cause the body to produce persistent insulin levels throughout the day. Insulin is a major hormone that signals the body to store fat. High sugar diets, or the consumption of cooked plant foods around the clock, force the body into a constant state of fat storage. The presence of insulin inhibits the body from tapping into fat stores for fuel and energy. Consuming pure animal fat creates no insulin response, and does not inhibit the body from tapping into it's own fat stores for energy.

The ketogenic diet, or a fat-adapted metabolism, causes the body to use fatty tissues for fuel, and allows mitochondria in fat cells to respirate. When mitochondria in fat cells respire, it means they can be used for fuel and energy. This creates higher energy levels and greater mental clarity. The body shifts from a state of fat-storage to one of fat-burning for fuel. This creates optimal physical and mental functioning as intended by nature.

I in no way advocate for the use of ketogenic diets for all people, especially women and children. Ketogenic diets are weight-loss diets, that optimize mental and physical performance. They are not for building and developing strong bodies, but are far better than vegan diets. They are excellent for the obese, over-weight, or metabolically deranged. **Individuals are unique and need varying levels of carbohydrates, proteins and fats depending on their goals, age, and constitutions.**

Our Paleolithic ancestors did not have food around the clock. The men often went for days without eating and were able to sustain themselves by tapping into their own fat stores for fuel. During hunts, women would often gather wild vegetation such as tubers to sustain and nourish the village.[10]

In Paleolithic cultures where food was not available for days, the men had the ability to endure long hunts without fatigue and energy crashes. This was due to their natural diets, which included ample amounts of animals fats in addition to the seasonal plant foods or carbohydrates that were available. The women gathered wild plants which were consumed by primarily by the women and children, but these plants were not the refined carbohydrates we consume today. They were tough, fibrous plants, that were properly prepared and processed. Further, they were not available around the clock, were mineral dense, and only available in season.

---

[10] Tedx Talks, Hunter-Gatherers, Human Diet, and Our Capacity for Cooperation/Alyssa Crittenden.

What has made us fat and obese are the same foods which cause every autoimmune disease and metabolic disorder. It is not the conventional energy balance hypothesis that thinks of a calorie as a calorie. This is a flawed argument with no scientific basis. What had made us fat, sick and obese, is consuming unnatural amounts of sub-optimal fuels in the form of carbohydrates, totally unprecedented in the history of our evolution. Everything from acne to cancer can be linked to the unnatural, over-consumption, of plant foods.

The energy balance theory proposes that sedentary lifestyles and over eating are a cause for obesity. Overweight medical patients are often told to just eat less. The idea of overeating calories being the cause of obesity is a baseless argument, totally ignorant of nutritional anthropology. Isolated cultures who enjoyed sedentary lifestyles with abundance of food, experience no such obesity. Modern people consume plant foods with no nutrients, and are thus starving and always craving more foods.

In most isolated and preindustrial cultures, meat and plant foods were abundant, and sedentary lifestyles were very common. Activities of preindustrial cultures primarily consisted of an occasional hunt, gathering wild foods, and artistic productions of ornaments, clothing, textiles and rugs. Conversely, there are ample examples of isolated cultures, who had their way of life destroyed by industrialization. These cultures became under-nourished, poor, lived very laborious lives, and yet suffered from obesity. Some examples of these cultures are the Pima Indians and The Sioux Indians.

The Pima Indians are a Native American tribe who's indigenous lands are in Arizona. In the 1840's they were recorded as being one of the most affluent Native American tribes. They lived as hunter-gatherers and also led an agrarian lifestyle. A few of the many plants they grew were wheat and beans. They also raised pig and cattle. They were recorded by an an American Army battalion who were passing through their territory, as being in remarkable health with an abundance of food.

During the gold rush in California between 1850 and 1880, many Americans traveled west towards California and across their territory. The U.S. Government asked the Pima Indians to feed and shelter American travelers across the southwest, due to their excessive reserves of food, and fertile land, which could sustain travelers.

By the end of the gold rush, the Pima lands were overwhelmed and destroyed by settlers who were moving west across their territory. All the of the wild game was hunted in the area and the Pima River which irrigated Pima lands, was diverted to irrigate the lands of the new European settlers. By 1902, The Pima were essentially starving and were recorded by Harvard anthropologist Frank Grasso, as living in poor conditions with a high prevalence of obesity. They went from being strong, healthy and fit, with an abundance of food, to poor, malnourished, starving and obese.

The Sioux Indians of South Dakota Crow Creek Reservation, were recorded by The University of Chicago to be living in "poor conditions beyond imagination". The Sioux lived on bread and coffee, yet obesity levels were similar to current Western industrialized peoples. They also had a prevalence of children who were very thin due to lack of nourishment.

In the 1960's, Trinidad was facing a severe malnutrition crisis. The United States sent a team of nutritionist to help them. They found that 1 in 3 women, over 25 were obese. The nutritional data from the country was studied by MIT and found that the women were all on a low-fat diet but consumed approximately 2,000 calories per day.

These populations were non-sedentary. They did not have couches and TV's like we do today. They were undernourished in terms of nutrition, had access to refined carbohydrates and yet obese. The calorie theory does not explain these cases. **The causes of obesity are malnourishment of fat-soluble vitamins, which allow the body to tap into its own fat reserves for energy, as well as inflammation due to carb-based diets and metabolic disorder.**

"A few years ago, I was visiting a primary care clinic in the slums of Sao Paulo (Brazil). The waiting room was full of mothers with thin, stunted young children, exhibitions of the typical signs of chronic undernutrition. There what might come as a surprise, is that many of the mothers holding those under-nourished infants were themselves overweight...The coexistence of underweight and overweight poses a challenge to public health programs, since the aims of programs to reduce undernutrition are obviously in conflict with those for obesity prevention."-Benjamin Caballero, John Hopkins University

Majority of overweight and obese people try counting calories to lose weight, but to no avail. They try eating less and exercising vigorously, which also doesn't work. The problem is not laziness or overeating, it is metabolic disorder. These individuals need to feed their body's fat in order to heal and to tap into their body's fat reserves. A body which does not receive proper nutrition in the form of animal, perceives that it is in an environment where food is scarce, and refuses to burn fat-stores.

It is unfortunate, that for nearly a century, patients have been blamed for obesity and told the culprit is their laziness and so called gluttony. The culprits are the USDA guidelines and medical advice. The foundation of the food pyramid is 5 to 11 servings of inflammatory carbohydrate foods, such as rice, wheat, potatoes, cereals and breads. This is inhumane at best and today is exasperated further with vegan diets.

For as long as obese people follow the advice of the USDA food pyramid, they will remain obese as such. Everytime carbohydrates are consumed and insulin raised, it will inhibit the release of fatty acids from storage. The body is handicapped from burning and utilizing it's own fat stores on high carb or plant based diets.

Children and babies grow rapidly not so much due to overeating, but due to hormonal signals secreted by their bodies. The hormonal profile of children include high insulin levels, which signal for the body to grow and accumulate fat. When carbohydrates and sugar are constantly consumed in vegan and standard American eaters, they are subject to chronically high levels of insulin, resulting in an amalgamation of fat storage. When insulin is down, ketones and fatty acids are mobilized from fat storage sites. Additionally, insulin is a key hormone which drives the aging process.

"Release of fatty acids from fat cells requires only the negative stimulus of insulin deficiency."-Rosalyn Yalow, Solomon Berson, 1965.

In the 1940's, the medical establishment understood that the proper diet for obesity was a low-carb diet, but due to the unfounded attacks on saturated fats by the pharmaceutical and seed-oil industry, animal fats were thrown out of favor through a meticulous propaganda campaign. There is enormous corruption, inconsistency and perversion of medicine and nutrition, prevalent in the United States today.

Metabolically adapting to fat burning for fuel, as opposed to sugar burning, is the single greatest health enhancer one could afford oneself of. It is only possible by consuming animal fats or fasting. When we fast, we essentially are consuming our own animal fat for fuel.

Our ancestors were hunter-gatherers who subsisted off of very fibrous plant foods until they caught a hunt. Women often gathered wild plants while men hunted. Carbohydrates were and have been an essential part of the diet, just like animal foods are. However, the problem today is that refined, hybridized carbohydrates, dominate the food pyramid, while nutrient-dense animals foods are minuscule or are all together neglected, such as in vegan diets.

An analogy first shared by Nora Gedguadas is perhaps the best way to explain the metabolic differences between fat and sugar for the laymen. She compared metabolism to the burning of a campfire, which I thought captured the essence of dietary macronutrient proportions perfectly.

Burning simple sugars can be thought of as kindle for fire. They provide small sparks that are highly flammable, and cause bursts of energy. The sugars or kindle, are honey, fruits and fruit juices, or any form of refined sugar. Constantly consuming these foods causes explosive burst of energy in the body which are harmful, although in proper portions they can serve to stoke metabolic fire.

Complex carbs can be likened to twigs. These include rice, beans, pasta and potatoes. They provide additional fuel to the fire, but are also burnt up rapidly and need constant maintenance in order to sustain the fire. They help to build up the strength of the fire from mere kindling, but also need constant replenishment. This is why vegans are always hungry, the food sources are burnt up quickly.

Animal proteins and fats are larger logs which burn for much longer periods of time. When animal foods are thrown on the metabolic fire, they offer steady, sustainable fuel. This steady fuel, requires of us to eat less and go on with our days. We are not subject to constant high and low blood sugar. This steady, sustainable fuel is also most optimal for the body. The burning of animal fat creates the least amount of metabolic waste, where as sugars and carbohydrates create far more waste products such as advanced glycation end products. Animal fats and proteins do not wrinkle skin and damage the organs when burnt for fuel the way sugars do.

Ideal metabolic health is achieved when one can manage a sustainable, strong, steady, and consistent fire, which needs minimal tending. To build a healthy fire, it requires all constituents in proper proportions. With only kindling, twigs and sticks (vegan diets) you must constantly feed the fire and suffer reoccurring spurts of low and high energy. This translates as constantly having to eat in order to regulate blood sugar, which is so common in most industrialized people.

The carbohydrates are burnt up quickly, leaving the person fatigued, hungry and tired. When logs, or protein and fat are placed in the fire, it allows for a steady, calm and long burning fire to take hold. This steady energy can sustain us for many hours without the need to constantly eat, and suffer from energy spikes and falls. Diabetes, which is a disease of blood sugar irregularities, is entirely caused by over indulgence of carbohydrates.

In wild nature, only ruminants and hind-gut fermenters subsist off of carbohydrates. The carbohydrates they consume are also absorbed as saturated fat and proteins, due to their digestive capacities. Nonetheless, they are forced to graze twelve plus hours a day in order to meet nutritional requirements. We humans are thinking creatures, capable of creating wondrous works of art and great civilizations. We are not meant to be preoccupied with eating food every two hours.

Fat is not only a fuel, but it builds our very structure and tissue, our hormones and organs. Only what is left over gets used as fuel. Fat is so important, that the body will use fuel from carbohydrates to form saturated fat and cholesterol, however there is a major difference between dietary fat, and fat obtained from carbohydrates via the liver.

When fat is obtained through animal foods, they come with their corresponding fat-soluble vitamins. This builds healthy subcutaneous fat, otherwise known as thick skin, in all the areas of the body, which is indicative of fertility and robustness. It builds thick, hydrated skin, and concentrates on the buttocks, hips and breast for women. It concentrates on the chest and shoulders for men.

When fat is obtained by way of carbohydrate consumption, it does not come with fat-soluble, body-building vitamins, and instead forms layers of fat which are designed for periods of famine and starvation. The fat is layered on the belly, arms and thighs, and is usually associated with cellulite and stretch marks. It is a sub-par fat. It does not moisturize or hydrate skin. It does not feed, build and moisturize internal organs.

Carbohydrates are stored as body fat in areas of the body which are not as desirable long-term, and associated with metabolic disorders. In the short-term, fat accumulation from carbohydrates is beneficial in specific circumstances. **Soon to be mothers, pregnant mothers, nursing mothers, and developing children, do need properly prepared carbohydrates in order to aid in healthy**

pregnancies, and the proper development of children. Please don't confuse my work in this book for carnivore or no carb diets. The need for low inflammatory carbohydrates varies by individuals and circumstances. My emphasis is the need for the inclusion of animal fat, and the proper understanding and context plant foods have in the diet. For the metabolically deranged, it is suitable to remove far more carbohydrates from the diet and pursue ketogenic diets, in order to regain metabolic balance. Developing children and pregnant mothers have different nutritional requirements than the metabolically deranged.

Individuals who are able to introduce animal fats into their diets, can obtain a high level of metabolic flexibility, as oppose to vegans who restrict animal foods. Metabolic flexibility allows us to maintain constant energy levels, with or without food, in a fasted state, as well as consume carbohydrates with negligible effects.

I do not advocate going zero-carb or forcing oneself into ketosis. I have seen too many cases of severe reactions by individuals who try to radically change their diets, especially women. Instead, individuals should simply add and include small amounts of animals fats into their diets, while reducing refined carbohydrates and empty calories. Overtime this will yield the best results, and without any of the potential consequences of shifting the metabolism and diet too drastically.

The modern body's of industrialized peoples which have been raised off of carbohydrates and refined sugars for the entirety of their lives, are addicted to carbs the way drugs addicts are to drugs. It is dangerous and irresponsible to remove the drug abruptly and completely at once. This would cause major upheavals in the body and brain's constitution.

The drug should be weened off of and the body supported by small amounts of fat-soluble vitamins, in the form of pastured butter, pastured fatty cuts of meats, and pastured eggs. It takes time for the body to remember how to properly metabolize and digest animal fats. There are very many reports amongst women who pursue ketogenic and low-carb diets for weight loss, but who suffer from some severe side effects.

Though they do accomplish their stated weight loss goals, it very common to also hear of anecdotal stories about the side effects of rapid dietary changes into ketoogenic diets, which can include hypo or hyper-thyroidism, autoimmunity, hair loss, and fatigue most often. I can not stress enough how important it is to work with the body, and do things in a slow, thoughtful and considerate manner.

Although I personally felt the initial brain building, energy giving and nerve soothing benefits, of animal fats immediately after reintroducing them into my diet, I was always riddled with some fatigue after consuming a steak or large meat meal. It was not until many months after, that I noticed the additional benefits associated with the fat-soluble vitamins. I am able to maintain muscle mass without exercise, sleep well, and have an incredible sense of well-being. It personally took me two years to be able to absorb and digest animal fats properly, without much fatigue. To this day, four years after coming off of a vegan diet and reintroducing nutrient-dense animal foods, I still notice monthly improvements in my absorption and utilization of animal fats.

Many individuals who would include some nutrient-dense animal fats into their diet will initially experience symptoms of nausea and fatigue. This is especially true in ex-vegans who have completely wrecked their metabolism and digestive tracts. It is important to understand here that animal foods are not explosive sugars or undigestible plant fibers. **This is real food which requires real digestion by the body.**

Think of the lions, and their days long bouts of lounging in the grasslands under trees, after consuming a fresh kill. It is normal to want to rest after the consumption of meat meals. With time, the body adapts and gets better at digesting the meat. Unlike the so called "adaptive phase" with veganism, which never really ends, the initial reintroduction and consumption of meat does not cause inflammation, nor gas, or bloating, the way plants do. There is an amalgamation of positive benefits that will occur with time after the introduction of animal fats into the diet.

CHAPTER 10

The Cholesterol, Saturated Fat & Heart-Disease Myth

The idea that dietary saturated fat and cholesterol cause heart disease is a myth, a financial scam, a farce, and a cruel conspiracy, percolated onto the public for the sake of corporate profits. There has been no other topic which has garnered as much money, study and attention, than the subject of saturated fat and heart-disease. Yet, time and time again the studies prove there is no correlation between the consumption of animal fats and heart disease.

The United States Food and Drug Administration has for decades, advised the public to lower blood cholesterol levels by reducing saturated fat in the diet. Public health agencies have also advocated for the use of statin drugs, high carbohydrate and low-fat diets, which are extremely inflammatory and are amongst the true culprits for heart-disease. They have failed to eradicate heart-disease which has now become a national endemic. **The first reported heart-attack in The United States was in 1921. Currently, there are 700,000 reported heart attacks yearly.**

There is very robust data and science which shows that there is absolutely no association between saturated animals fats with heart-disease, and type 2 diabetes. In fact, the studies show the opposite, that saturated fat is protective of heart-disease. The real problem has always been inflammatory, unnatural foods, such as refined carbohydrates, breads, pastas, cereals, seed oils and sugar, the very foundation of the USDA food pyramid and vegan diets. It is inflammation which damages the arteries. Saturated fat is the least inflammatory food. It is the food we were meant to consume. It is the foods of modern commerce and industrialization which are entirely new additions to the human diet and which exasperate heart-disease and nearly every other disorder.

The foundation of the cholesterol-saturated-fat-heart-disease myth, rests on the flawed science of a biochemist in the 1950's, named Ansel Keys. Ansel Keys published a study that correlated fat consumption with heart disease in six countries. He concluded, that heart disease was correlated with the amount of saturated fat consumption in a given society. The issue with his hypothesis was that it was completely bias. He left out countries in which there were very high amounts of saturated fat consumption and very little heart disease, such as Holland and Norway.

He also excluded countries where there was very little saturated fat consumption but a high prevalence of heart disease, such as Chile. He had reliable data from 22 countries but omitted that vast majority of them when he published his results. The reason for his omission of the data was because they did not fit the narrative of his state and corporate sponsors, who had an agenda to demonize saturated fats before the study even commenced.

It should be understood by the reader, that the majority of science conducted in the industrialized nations of the world today, is junk science. 95% of the nutritional studies are funded by the pharmaceutical and petrochemical agricultural industries. There are independent research labs across the country, that are contracted by corporations to perform studies on their behalf. These independent labs openly advertise that they can manipulate data and publish studies showing whatever the corporation is set out to prove. There is hardly any real, objective science today. **We can find a study to prove and disprove almost anything.**

Shortly after Ansel Keys published his data, he received a picture on time magazine and became the father of what would be called, "The Lipid Hypothesis". This hypothesis states, that eating saturated fat, raises cholesterol levels and causes heart-disease. The hypothesis was immediately adopted by the State, the medical establishment, the pharmaceutical industry, and the petrochemical agricultural industry. The pubic was advised to cut their consumption of saturated animal fats in favor of grains and seed-oils, cultivated by the mega-food and petrochemical corporations. They were also encouraged to take statins in order to lower cholesterol. This hypothesis proved to be very lucrative, and was to provide these industries with a very large populace of grain eating, sick and diseased people.

"The hypothesis that when you eat high fat, that then produces high cholesterol and the cholesterol produces heart disease, is wrong in every one of those legs."- Al Sears, M.D.

"This whole idea that dietary fat causes cholesterol problems is sort of a myth. The whole idea that the cholesterol problem leads to heart disease is a myth."- Michael R. Eades, M.D.

"The theory is completely and totally wrong. It was a theory that was made out of whole cloth and then pushed."- Mary Enig, Ph.D., biochemist and author of, *Know Your Fats*

Many brilliant physicians, Ph.D's, authors, and researchers, have performed a considerable amount of research on this topic, and read through the medical literature. A few of them are:

- Uffe Ravnskov, MD, PhD and author of *The Cholesterol Myths; Exposing the Fallacy that Saturated fat and Cholesterol Cause Heart Disease.*
- Investigative science and health journalist Gary Taubes published *Good Calories-Bad Calories.*
- Malcom Kendrick MD authored *The Great Cholesterol Con.*
- Stephen Sinatra, M.D, F.A.C.C. and Johny Bowden, Ph.D., C.N.S. coauthored *The Great Cholesterol Myth; Why Lowering Your Cholesterol Wont Prevent Heart Disease*

When these researchers, physicians, and authors, analyzed all the data on heart-disease, they found that there were **ZERO** studies that proved that a diet high in animal fat causes heart-disease.

Since 1948, The Harvard Medical School has been following the diets and death rates of the entire population of Framingham, Massachusetts. The study is one of the largest ever conducted. One of the researchers involved in The Framingham study said of the lipid-hypothesis or cholesterol-heart disease myth,

"The greatest scientific scam of this century, perhaps of any century."- George Mann, M.D., Framingham Study

The newest theories in heart disease have nothing to do with cholesterol or animal fats. They have to do with seed-oils, anti-nutrients or plant toxins, and sugars or carbohydrates, causing inflammation in the arteries. Animal fats are the least inflammatory foods. It is inflammation which damages arteries. Dietary inflammation is caused by eating an unnatural diet, and there is no diet as unnatural as the standard American or vegan diet.

The standard American and vegan diets rely almost entirely on carbohydrates, plant oils, frankenstein grains, and sugars. Vegans, vegetarians and those on the Standard American diet are subject to a constant onslaught of these inflammatory foods.

All people with heart-disease have signs of severe underlying inflammation. Inflammation is the root and cause of every degenerative disease, in conjunction with malnourishment and environmental toxicity. **The same foods which damage the intestinal-lining, are the very foods which damage the rest of the body, the arteries, the brain, the heart, the kidneys, the liver, and the pancreas. It is unfathomable to think that our natural diet could cause us harm.** In fact, it doesn't, as all the studies have shown, saturated fat does not cause heart-disease. The data shows those who consume the most carbohydrates and seed-oils, suffer from the highest incidence of heart-disease.

Heart-disease is caused primarily by plant foods in three ways. First, heart-disease develops when arteries are damaged by plant-toxins, such as those mentioned in chapter one. These plant toxins not only damage the gut-lining but also all cells they come into contact with, including the cells of the arteries. Second, excess carbohydrates consumption, blood sugar spikes, and the unregulated flow of sugar through the arteries, causes free-radical damage, bursting the cell membranes of arterial cell walls. Sugar literally flows through the arteries damaging and killing cells. The third way is when plant or seed-oils travel through the blood-stream causing oxidization of hardening of the arteries. Vegetable oil are not compatible with human physiology and harden in the body, unlike animal fats.

The body sends cholesterol, a healing substance, to the site of inflammation or damage. This commences the healing process. Just like a scab on the surface of the skin, which is wholly made of cholesterol, the body produces the same waxy substance to heal internal wounds. LDL is a protein used by the body to shuttle cholesterol to the site of injury, HDL proteins are used by the body to shuttle cholesterol from the site of injury back to the liver, to be recycled. LDL and HDL are proteins that carry cholesterol. Cholesterol is so precious and important to the body, that it recycles what it can for later use.

Calcification of the arteries occurs when sugars, plant-toxins, and seed-oils damage the arterial wall and harden cholesterol inside the artery. These toxic plant compounds cause cholesterol to harden. Sugars become like hardened crystal inside the arteries. The calcified cholesterol obstructs blood flow in the arteries and plaque begins to form. This leads to heart attacks. Cholesterol is merely the ambulance, the fire truck in the body, traveling to the site of inflammation, in order to repair and heal cells. Abnormal diets cause this cholesterol to harden and calcify, causing obstruction in the arterial walls.

The way to reverse the process is not by handicapping the body's ability to produce its own healing substance, cholesterol, by taking statins, but to quit consuming inflammatory foods which damage the arteries in the first place, such as excess sugars, plant-chemicals and seed-oils. Certain nutrients only found in pastured animal fats, such as K2 in butter and egg yolks, have been found to help the body to decalcify and heal arteries. There is nothing new under the sun.[11] Our natural diets always were the solution to great health and longevity.

---

[11] Hariri E, Kassis N, Iskandar J, *et al*, Vitamin K2—a neglected player in cardiovascular health: a narrative review. *Open Heart* 2021; 8: e001715. doi: 10.1136/openhrt-2021-001715.

Most Americans have been told to lower their cholesterol and take statins. They have also been told to go on plant-based or vegan diets in order to avoid cholesterol. I had elaborated on the need for high cholesterol and it's association with longevity in the previous chapters. The State and Corporate oligarchy is not only removing the most nutritious foods from the food pyramid, but are also advising the public to consume copious amounts of the most inflammatory and disease causing foods. To further cause injury to harm, they are actively disabling the body from being able to produce it's own cholesterol, it's own healing substance, through the widespread prescriptions of statins.

Are you beginning to grasp what has happened. The theory of animal foods contributing to cancer and heart-disease has had enormous financial gain for very powerful corporations. The mega petrochemical food cultivators get to sell us toxic seed-oils, in place of natural animal fats. They get to feed us the same way they feed a cage operated, factory farmed cattle. A diet high in frankenstein grains, seed-oils and sugars, produced in mass through tractors and petrochemicals. North America's illness's and diseases fill the pocket books of the pharmaceutical industry, which profits hundreds of billions of dollars a year, on a sick, malnourished population. Vegan and Standard American diets reap trillions of dollars of revenue for the corporate-oligarchy.

The lipid-hypothesis and cholesterol scare mongering has most adults convinced that they need to take a statin to prevent heart attacks. **Statins which are a cholesterol lowering drug are the number one drug sold on the planet. It is the most lucrative cash cow for the pharmaceutical industry.**

It is so important to emphasize here again, cholesterol is the greatest dietary nutrient. Cholesterol is the builder, lubricator, sustainer, fuel and detoxifier, of all bodily tissues. It heals all internal and external wounds. It gives strength and is needed for the development of all hormones and neurotransmitters. It is needed for proper brain function and thinking. To disable the body of it's ability to produce cholesterol, is to the disable the body from performing all of it's self regenerative, self sustaining functions. **This is exactly what statins do. They disable the body from producing it's own cholesterol.**

Recall what I wrote in the previous chapter about cholesterol being a crucial component of our brain and hormones. The number one side effect of statins is memory loss. A starving brain, a brain starving of cholesterol, can not function well and degenerates. Statins are causing a parkinson's, alzheimer's and dementia epidemic. 40% of the brain is cholesterol, and the medical establishment is prescribing senior citizens drugs which inhibits their body's production of cholesterol. Almost all senior citizens in nursing homes are prescribed statins.

The side effects associated with low cholesterol are:

- Increased risk of heart disease.
- Voilent suicide.
- Parkinsons, dementia, memory loss, learning disabilities.
- Associated with early death and premature aging.
- Increased risk of cancer and more.

"The diet-heart hypothesis we can 100% say has been proven wrong. The diet-heart hypothesis is a big mistake. It has been proven wrong for the last 30 years. But because our political and commercial machine has committed to this hypothesis, they work very hard not to allow the population to know the truth."- Dr. Natasha McBride MD, world renowned keynote speaker and author of, *Gut and Psychology Syndrome.*

CHAPTER 11

Government & Corporate Collusion, Dietary Propaganda & Statins

In light of the facts to animal fats and cholesterol, I must explain how and why the populace has been duped into such a con. Why has veganism risen so much in popularity as of late? What incentive did government agencies have to make ill their own population and profit at the demise of their health? The answer is always for financial reasons. A healthy, sane and vibrant population, does not serve the capitalistic interest of the corporate-oligarchy. The corporate-oligarchy has tremendous power in Washington through their lobbyist.

In 1988, The U.S. Department of Health and Human Services Surgeon General's Office, set out to prove Ansel Key's Lipid hypothesis by reviewing data from all the major studies available at that time. After 11 years and 100 million dollars, they found that the results of the data were not supportive of Ansel Key's Lipid-hypothesis theory. In turn, they shut down the entire project and blamed it on complications.

Over the decades, corporate and state sponsored researchers have routinely ignored and discarded evidence which contradicted the lipid-hypothesis theory. Very often, they would manipulate data in order to support the hypothesis. This type of dishonesty and corruption is rampant today in nutritional sciences.

In the 1970's, the lipid-hypothesis was still in dispute. A senate committee lead by Senator George Mcgovern was commissioned to settle the dispute. The committee had originally published a report urging Americans to cut down on consumption of cholesterol and dietary fat, in order to reduce the risk for heart-attacks. Eminent scientist of the time had rejected the committee's initial report. Prominent physicians across the nation took issue with that report, arguing that numerous studies failed to show hard evidence associating animal fat with heart-disease.

The senate committee led by George Mcgovern had decided to ostracize and exclude any and all scientists, researchers, and medical physicians, who opposed their views. The senate committee had the backing, funding and lobbying, of powerful agro-commodity and pharmaceutical corporations. It was essentially a sell out.

The committee, on behalf of corporate financial interest, recommended a low-fat, high grain and carbohydrate diet, for the whole of the population. Soon after, the USDA got involved and issued a high carbohydrate, high sugar and high grain diet, as official government policy. A handful of politicians with no background or interest in nutritional sciences, along with their corporate sponsors, had subjected The American public, to a decades long, unwitting science experiment.

Instead of serving the health and interest of the public, politicians yield to corporate donors, sponsors and lobbyist. There should be nothing shocking about that statement. America is a capitalistic society. Capitalism prioritizes industry, financials, and gross domestic product, before anything else. The health of the public is not even a consideration.

Large multi-national corporations who have roots in the pharmaceutical and chemical industries, control official government agricultural, dietary, and nutritional policy. A few of these companies are Dupont, Monstanto and Syngenta, amongst many more. These corporations essentially control the food supply and majority of the grains, seed-oils and carbohydrate foods fed to not only Americans, but much of the world. Pastured animal products come from family farms and not multi-national, mega-food corporations. A low animal-fat, high carbohydrate, or vegan diet, is in the financial interest of the large multinational corporations.

In conjunction with ill-advised and ill-intentioned dietary recommendations, large pharmaceutical corporations profit immensely with the lipid-hypothesis, or the cholesterol heart-disease theory. Statins, which are again designed to handicap the body's ability to produce cholesterol, are the most widely prescribed drug in the world. **If the public were to lose their fear of cholesterol, the pharmaceutical industry would lose the revenue of their best selling drug.**

Since the introduction of statins in the 1980's, they have been the most lucrative class of drugs for the pharmaceutical industry. Large pharmaceutical giants such as Pfizer and AstraZeneca have profited in trillions of dollars in revenue due to statins. Statin drugs are the most profitable drug in the history of medicine, with total annual sales exceeding one-trillion dollars in revenue. If the public were to understand the con and quit their fear of saturated animal fat and dietary cholesterol, it could collapse the US economy due to windfall against the major pharmaceutical corporations. The economic well being of The United States depends of the public being in poor health and subject to psychological manipulation.

If you actually look into the data and statistics on statins, you find that they virtually offer no protection against heart-attacks. The pharmaceutical industrial complex advertised statins to the public with claims that statins such as lipitor, reduce heart-attacks by 50%. This is a pathetic distortion of the data. When compared against placebo groups, statins show to have virtually no difference in rates of heart-attacks, yet with a plethora of adverse effects.

The most common side effects of statins are type two diabetes and dementia. **It is interesting to note, that all statins have a little disclosure on the package claiming that they have not been shown to prevent heart-disease or heart-attacks.** The side effects of the statins and cholesterol lowering drugs include everything from degenerative brain diseases to osteoporosis, depression, and suicide. This should come as no surprise to readers as I have already belabored on the importance of cholesterol in the body.

Scientist and researchers who do not fall in line with government policy, have their funding and credentials rebuked. There is immense economic pressure at The National Institute of Health and their research labs, which live off of government funding to perpetuate the official narrative. Eminent researchers such as Dr. Kilmer McCully MD, who go against the prevailing theory, have their careers sabotaged. He published a study at Harvard University concluding something other than cholesterol was causing heart disease. As a result of his publication, he was denied tenure, lost all of his research grants, and was listed on an unofficial blacklist. The evidence against the cholesterol-heart disease myth is overwhelming.

"The diet-heart hypothesis has been repeatedly shown to be wrong, and yet for complicated reasons of pride, profit, and prejudice, the hypothesis continues to be exploited by scientist, fund-raising enterprises, food companies and even governmental agencies. The public is being deceived by the greatest health scam of the

century." -Dr. George Mann, MD, Associate Director of The Framingham Heart Study

CHAPTER 12

Toxic Vegetable-oils Replacing Nourishing Animal Fats

In place of natural animal fats, vegan advocates, the USDA, and other government agencies, have advocated for the use of commercially produced seed-oils in the diets of Americans. Their use was encouraged through well funded, well organized, large-scale, public relations campaigns, that were designed to manipulate public opinion on saturated animal fats. The public growing weary of animal fats, began to consume seed-oils in large quantities, instead of animal fats that had been used since the beginning of human history. The public relations campaign also cleverly referred to these seed-oils as vegetable oils, in an attempt to paint a healthy picture over them. In this chapter, I will refer to them as seed-oils, because that is what they really are.

The most common seed-oils are corn oil, cotton seed oil, soybean oil, safflower oil, peanut oil and canola oil. These oils are used in almost every singe packaged and refined food, as well as in most restaurants and kitchens in North America. Prior to the advent of seed oils, fats such as lard, tallow and butter, were used for cooking unanimously across the world. Nearly all the shelves inside of a grocery store have packaged foods which include high fructose corny syrup and one of the refined seed-oils mentioned above. These seed-oils are a new introduction to the human diet and have replaced animal fats humans have used since the dawn of our history, such as tallow, lard, suet and butter.

When seed-oils were initially introduced on the market in the late 1800's, they were used as lubricants for industrial machinery during the industrial-revolution. They were never intended for human consumption. Due to the chemical fatty acid composition of seed-oils, they are incompatible with human physiology. The body can not properly use them for fuel, lubrication, moisturization, detoxification, and building material for cellular membranes. They are inferior to animal fats. They cannot even be compared to animal fats.

I will attempt to summarize the chemical differences between animal fats and seed-oils in a very condensed manner. Seed-oils have double bonds between carbon molecules which do not allow the lipid molecules to sit on top of each other, and create a solid food. There is space between the molecules in oils. Animal fats have no such double bond between the carbon molecule, which allow their lipids to sit flat on top of one another, creating a solid food, such a butter or meat fat.

In order for seed-oils to be used as foods, the seed-oil industry manipulates their chemistry through a process called hydrogenation. Hydrogenation is a very complex process that involves many steps carried out by machinery. It involves the application of pressure and heat from machines, and hexane solvents, which extracts a rancid, grey, unpalatable liquid or oil. The oil is further winterized and deodorized to become stable. It is not a simple process such as milking a cow and churning butter. This industrial process allowed seed oils to enter the food market.

Seed oils were initially sold as soap by Proctor & Gamble until Cisco advertised it as a commercial food product in 1911. The seed-oil industry launched a baseless public relations campaign claiming that seed-oils were "new, modern and healthy". Their intention was to convince the public to substitute seed-oils in place of animal fats for cooking. Later, margarine entered the market which is a hardened vegetable oil.

Prior to the advent of these-seed oils, heart-disease was virtually unknown. It was not until these seed-oils were introduced into the human diet in 1911, that we find a sharp uptick in heart-disease, which has turned into a full blown epidemic over the coarse of the 20th century. The rise in heart disease correlates perfectly with the introduction of seed-oils into the human diet. Our consumption of polyunsaturated seed-oils went from 0 to 80 grams a day over the coarse of the 20th century. This is one of the single greatest changes to human nutrition in all of our history.

By 1961, the seed-oil industry had gained significant influence and power over both, the public and politicians in Washington. Procter & Gamble, an American multinational consumer goods corporation and producer of seed-oils, launched The American Heart Association (AHA). In turn the American Heart Association advertised seed-oils as a health food on behalf of Proctor & Gamble. The AHA has deep ties with with industrial seed-oil industry. The AHA recommended that all Americans replace their animal fats with seed-oils, in order to fight heart-disease.

The recommendation was never based on science, but on industry and lobbying. Since the inception of The AHA and their recommendations, there has been a marked increase in heart-attacks in parallel with seed-oil consumption, and diminishment of saturated fat in the diet. One can not be shocked to learn of such things, in a capitalistic society, it is the health of the economy and financial growth which are prioritized, not the health of the pubic.

The hypothesis of replacing saturated fats with polyunsaturated fats or seed-oils, has been tested in large, randomized, controlled, clinical trials, on more people then ever have been tested on any other hypothesis in the world of nutritional science. The results are always the same. There is no effect of saturated animal fats on cardiovascular mortality. This knowledge is totally ignored by vegan doctors and nutritionist, as well as Public Health Agencies.

In these trials, animal fats are replaced with seed-oils such as canola, soybean or cotton-seed oil. The studies set out to observe the results of what a high seed-oil diet would yield, and the results are always worrisome. In a six year study called "The LA Veterans Study", 850 elderly men were placed on high seed-oil diets. Those placed on the high seed-oil diet died of two times the rate of cancer, than the group who were still consuming animal fats. Other side effects include increased risk of stroke, heart attack and gallstones.[12]

Hydrogenated seed-oils, in addition to wheat and refined sugars, such as high fructose corn syrup, have become the backbone of the commercial food industry. Every packaged and processed food in a grocery store aisle is composed of sugar, grain and a seed-oil. These ingredients are used in every chip, cookie, cereal, cracker, cake, candy and more. These ingredients are all also considered vegan. It is not hard to see that Americans are already largely on a plant-based diet. The transition to veganism is merely giving up their drive thru burgers and chicken nuggets, which can hardly be called nutritious animal foods.

The introduction of all of these non-foods into the human diet, and then encouraging them to be the foundation of dietary habits, is an experiment on human health which obviously has had severe repercussions. It is

---

[12] A Controlled Clinical Trial of a Diet High in Unsaturated Fat. Preliminary observations, S DAYTON, M L PEARCE, S HASHIMOTO, L J FAKLER, E HISCOCK, W J DIXON. PMID: 13884081.

absurd to think that by pressing seed-oils through industrial machinery, we could replace the animal fats we have been consuming for all of our human history.

In many non-industrialized cultures around the world today, they understand that seed-oils are far inferior to animal fats when used for cooking. In The Caucuses, Central Asia and other less industrialized parts of the world, it is still commonly understood that those individuals who consume and use industrial seed-oils in place of animal fats, do not properly develop, are weak, frail, and less resilient to disease, than those who grew up consuming traditional native fats. Part of the reason is because seed-oils are completely lacking in bodybuilding, fat-soluble vitamins that are found in animal fats, in addition to oxidative damage that seed-oils subject the body to.

Seed-oils are susceptible to rancidity and oxidization. This means they oxidize and rust just like iron does when exposed to moister and air. They are no where near as stable as animal fats. The consumption of seed-oils causes the cellular membranes of our body to be made of oxidized fats. These rancid fats accumulate and store in the body over time. This is important as researchers have found that the nature of bodily fatty acid composition, has a strong association with longevity. When animal cells are made of fatty acids which are hard to oxidize, such as those fats found in saturated animal fats, they live longer. Conversely, when they are made up of oxidized, polyunsaturated fatty acids from seed-oils, the animals suffer shorter life spans.

"Saturated and monounsaturated fatty acids are very resistant to peroxidative damage, while the more polyunsaturated a fatty acid, the more susceptible it is to peroxidation. Furthermore, the products of lipid peroxidation can oxidatively damage other important molecules. Membrane fatty acid composition is correlated with the maximum lifespans of mammals and

birds. Exceptionally long-living mammal species and birds have a more peroxidation-resistant membrane composition compared to shorter-living similar-sized mammals. Within species, there are also situations in which extended longevity is associated with peroxidation-resistant membrane composition."- *Explaining Longevity of Different Animals: Is Membrane Fatty Acid Composition the Missing Link?* A.J. Hulbert.

The percentage of polyunsaturated seed-oils in peoples fat cells have gradually made up larger portions of cellular membranes. In fact, it has doubled from 10% in 1960 to around 20% in 2005. The concentration of polyunsaturated fatty acids from seed-oils in isolated and non-industrialized cultures is less than 4%. Today, we are placed on abnormal, plant-based diets which shorten our lifespan. To live to 100 was normal in most isolated and pre-industrialized culture. Today, North Americans can hardly reach the age of 60.

I personally knew a man who was attempting to subsist on a vegan diet despite marked evidence of failure. He became frail, weak and extremely ill looking. He attempted multiple different vegan diets in order to regain health. After failing on a whole-foods vegan diet, he transitioned and attempted a vegan ketogenic diet.

He thought that he could replicate a natural ketogenic metabolism on a vegan diet using plant oils as his source of fat. He was consuming upwards of a cup of organic olive oil a day for fuel. When I encountered him during his experiment, I was sure that I had never before encountered such a sickly looking individual in my life. Even the worse drug addicts seemed healthier than him. He could barely walk fifteen feet before becoming extremely fatigued. He could not formulate sentences, was completely spaced out, and seemed on the verge of death. I witness him grabbing his chest several times, as if he were on the verge of a heart attack.

I pleaded with him to give up his vegan diet and return to a traditional way of eating. He could not accept the fact that his diet was harming him. He could not open his mind to new possibilities, and even became defensive when I tried having a conversation with him about his diet. It was very evident that his brain was starving of cholesterol and saturated fat. He had every indication of extreme brain starvation and looked incredibly ill.

The highest quality, cold-pressed, organic polyunsaturated seed-oils, go rancid merely by sitting in a bottle on the store shelf. When they go through the industrial process needed to extract the oil from the seed, they rapidly oxidize due to the heat and solvents needed to extract the oil. They also continue to oxidize or go rancid, while sitting in the body. The oxidation process leads to very large amounts of aldehydes in the oil. Aldehyde levels in the body are a formal marker for cancer risk. Aldehydes are known to cause rapid cell death, disturb DNA and RNA, and inhibit proper cell function. They also have very high levels of free radicals.

When seed-oils are processed, they have hydrogen molecules broken off, and in essence what you have is sharp daggers in the chemistry. This creates additional free radical damage in the body when consumed, causing cuts and legions in arteries, and systemic cellular damage. This increases cancers, heart disease, premature aging, immune system dysfunction, depressed learning ability, liver damage, reproductive organ damage, digestive disorders, impaired growth and lower cholesterol.

According to vegans, as well as corporate and government diet-dictators, saturated animal fats are a new addition to our diet, and are the reason why we have so much heart-disease, cancer and diabetes. Such baseless claims are made in hopes that we will have no understanding of cultural and dietary anthropology, ancestral cultures, agricultural anthropology, nutrition, metabolism, human digestion, physiology and so on.

Over 100 years ago, before the advent of industrial seed-oils into the market, every recipe globally included saturated animal fat for cooking, and heart-disease was a non-issue. Seed-oils did not exist. With the introduction of commercial seed-oils into the diet, heart-disease skyrocketed.

US Deaths Due to Heart Disease- (1900-2011)

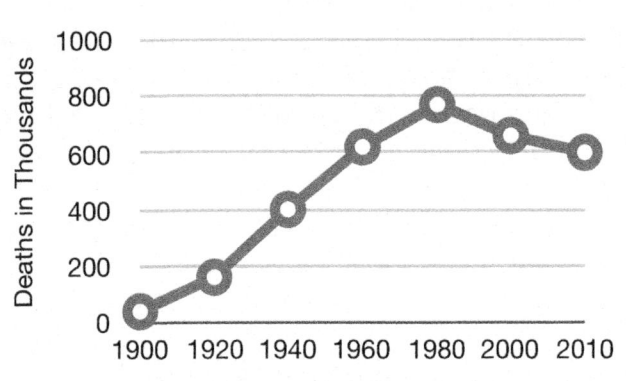

Year (Source : National Center for Health Statistics)

The heart disease epidemic is directly correlated with the manipulation of the food supply by corporate interest and their government cronies. Keep in mind, industrial seed-oils were first introduced into the diet of Americans in 1911. Since that time, massive public relation's campaign have been launched by vegan zealots, government agencies, and seed-oil producing corporations, advocating for the removal of animal fat from the diet and the inclusion of their rancid, unnatural seed oils.

Even with the obvious demise of the public's health since the introduction of these seed-oils, the medical establishment continues to insist that saturated fats are the cause of heart-disease. The issue is getting worse in current times as gullible youth further pedal malnourishing diets such as veganism, unwittingly on behalf of very powerful, multinational corporations, who profit immensely on the sales of their petrochemical, agricultural products.

The saturated-fat-heart-disease con, has meet very stiff resistance over the years. An important figure who offered resistance to their campaigns was Dr. Paul Dudley White MD, who is often considered the father of modern cardiology. He was vehemently opposed to seed or vegetable-oils, and encouraged the use of eggs, fatty meat, lard and butter. He was responsible for introducing the cardiogram to America and was also President Eisenhower's personal physician.

"See here, I began my practice as a cardiologist in 1921 and I never saw an MI patient (myocardial infarction) until 1928. Back in the MI free days, before 1920, the fats were butter and lard, and I think we would all benefit from the kind of diet we had at that time, when no one had heard the word corn oil." -Paul Dudley White MD, The Father of Modern Cardiology

The edible seed-oil industry is one of the contributing forces responsible for the decay and corruption rampant in Washington, and for the perversion of nutritional sciences. They have a very powerful lobby in Washington D.C. called The Institute for Shortening and Edible Oils (ISEO). This lobby has worked behind the scenes with public relations campaigns and lobbying politicians, for the purpose of nationalizing their products into official government dietary guidelines, and to demonize the competition, which are animal fats.

By the 1960's, the seed-oil industry and their powerful lobby group gained enough influence and power to the point that they practically supervised The American Heart (AHA) Association, The National Heart, Lung, and Blood Institute (NHLBI), and The American Dietetic Association (ADA). They ensured that all of these organizations had board members in line with their agenda, promoting diets high in seed-oils and grains, and low in animal fat.

By 1971, The FDA's general counsel became president of the edible oil trade association, who was in turn replaced at the FDA by a food lawyer, Peter Barton Hatt of Covington & Burling, who represented the edible oil industry. In the 70's and 80's, Dr. Mattson from Proctor & Gamble, one of the largest producers of seed-oils, held multiple controlling positions in The Lipid Research Clinic Trials, that led to The National Cholesterol Education Program.

In essence, what we have is corporations dictating public health and nutritional policy according to their financial interest. The collusion between the State and enterprise in this manner is often referred to as the revolving door policy. It exist in nearly every aspect of government and industry. The very industries that our governments should be regulating and policing, are instead in charge of official government policy. They are all, without exception, motivated by profit.

In 1972, there was a concerted psychological warfare effort by The AHA, AMA and NAS, against The American Public. All three issued statements that were designed to scare Americans for their own financial motives. The official statements declared that Americans had cholesterol levels that were too high, and that it was important for Americans to lower cholesterol. They called for measuring cholesterol levels in all routine check-ups and physical examinations from early adulthood and onwards. They declared that Americans in "risk category" should receive "appropriate dietary advice", reduce saturated animal fat intake, and substitute them with vegetable-oils. They also called for all legal barriers and regulatory restrictions for the marketability and availability of packaged and processed foods with vegetable-oils to be removed. The American public became anxious and fearful about cholesterol, the most powerful and important substance within the human body.

At the time, there were very many critics, scientist and physicians, who opposed their views. To appease the critics, in 1984, the government and their corporate sponsors initiated "The 1984 Cholesterol Consensus Conference" and invited the opposition. The goal of the conference was to seem objective and impartial to the scientific findings on cholesterol and to discuss the science and facts. The dissenters were allowed to speak and express their views, however, their views were not included in the panel report. Even worse, the conclusion of the findings of the conference were written before the conference was even convened. The entire aim of the conference was to give the public the appearance as if they came to impartial, objective, and scientific conclusions on saturated fats, cholesterol and heart disease. The conclusion of the conference called for mass cholesterol screenings, diets low in saturated fat and cholesterol, and the replacement of butter with seed-oils and margarine.

The conclusion of the conference led to the launching of "The National Cholesterol Education Program", who's stated goal and aim was to change the attitudes of physicians on cholesterol and animal fats. At the time, there were still many physicians who were opposed to the corporate sponsored, seed-oil, and vegan agenda. By 1990, their consolidation over the nutritional and medical establishment came to a saturation point. **The National Institute of Health (NIH) recommended the prudent diet, a diet low in saturated animal fat, for all Americans over the age of two.**

The prudent diet has an interesting history, as research and data on the diet shows it is not beneficial for heart-disease, and yet is still peddled onto the public for the very reason of combating heart-disease. The prudent diet is embodied in the current USDA food pyramid but has recently been replaced for the more trendy vegan diet.

In 1957, The Anti-Coronary Club in New York led by Dr. Norman Joliffe, director of The Nutrition Bureau of The New York Health Department, commenced a study that placed a group of adult men between ages 40 and 59, on the prudent diet. Members of the prudent diet consumed corn oil and margarine instead of butter, and breakfast cereals in place of eggs, chicken, fish and beef. The prudent diet is essentially a vegan diet. There was a control group of the same age that consumed eggs for breakfast and meat three times a day.

The results were published in 1966, nine years after the study commenced. The results were published in the medical journal, "*Bulletin New York Academy of Medicine 1968*".
The experiment was purported to be a success because the men on the prudent diet had cholesterol levels lower than the men consuming animals fats. This premise alone should cast doubt on the study, due to the benefits of higher cholesterol levels which I explainer earlier. At the end of the journal, in very fine small print, there is a paragraph which states that the men on the prudent diet with lower cholesterol, suffered eight deaths from heart attacks, and the men in the control group with higher cholesterol and animal fat based diet, suffered from no heart attacks. Even

though the prudent members died of heart attacks, the diet is considered successful because they at least died with lower cholesterol levels.[13] This is insanity, it is not science.

Think of everything I have wrote in this book pertaining to the need the body has for saturated fat and cholesterol. The anthropology of human dietary and hunting practices, the nutritional content of foods, the inflammatory aspect of the carbohydrate and plant-based foods advocated by the government agencies, the need for higher cholesterol levels in order to sustain health, longevity and well-being. The establishment is telling us to do the exact opposite of what is good for us. This is beyond corruption and lack of integrity. It is a form of genocide and nutritional deprivation of The American People, imposed on us by way of national policy. Today, it is coming to a crescendo with absurd dietary trends such as veganism.

The very vitamins, minerals, and foods which contributed to human development, great civilizations, larger brains, great health, leisure, and in turn great works of art and science, are being eradicated from our diets in the name of health and sustainability.

The war on cholesterol and mass prescribing of statins is about incorporating otherwise healthy people into a ethic-less, medical system, and profiting on their ignorance. Once the body loses it's ability to produce it's own cholesterol due to statin drugs, it's degradation process speeds up rapidly. What were formerly healthy senior citizens, begin to suffer from aches, pains, dementia, and other disorders, making them vulnerable to a cocktail of medications ready to be prescribed to them. All of this is considered a success by the The State, as well as the medical and pharmaceutical establishment, because it

---

[13] Christakis, G et al. "The anti-coronary club. A dietary approach to the prevention of coronary heart disease--a seven-year report." *American journal of public health and the nation's health* vol. 56,2 (1966): 299-314. doi:10.2105/ajph.56.2.299

reflects a growth in medical expenses, and in turn gross domestic product. It is seen as a positive for the economy.

There are ample amounts of rodent studies which show that statins cause cancers in rodent models. These statins have systemic effects on the body. They not only inhibit cholesterol production, but block the absorption of fat-soluble vitamins and many minerals. The side effects include fatigue, weakness, memory loss, reduced mental capacity, muscle wasting, reduced libido, depression, suicide and cancer.[14]

We need cholesterol rich animal foods for longevity, health and well-being. They are not dispensable. They are a primary food, without which the human body falls apart. The same corporate and government institutions responsible for the ill-founded USDA food pyramid, are now at the helm of The Vegan Agenda.

Their has been immense profit in the destruction of the public's health. Industry has conspired to convince the populace that natural foods which mankind has sustained off of since the dawn of human history are dangerous and unhealthy. They have conspired to inoculate fear into the public's hearts, and change their perspective of their health and bodies. There is a general, subconscious anxiety, always at play in the psyches of industrialized people. A fear that the body is fundamentally flawed and subject to random diseases at anytime. They have been trained to always be under the constant watch and supervision of the medical establishment. To not trust in Nature, in God, or even themselves. Their critical thinking, feeling, and sensing faculties, have been neutered and they no longer know who or what to trust.

---

[14] Carcinogenicity of Lipid-Lowering Drugs. Thomas B. Newman, MD, MPH; Stephen B. Hulley, MD, MPH *JAMA*. 1996;275(1):55-60. doi:10.1001/jama.1996.03530250059028

In such an environment, medical doctors who parrot information are deemed father figures and guides, despite the fact that many have no understanding of nutrition or health themselves. The profession has degraded to little more than drug peddling. The medical profession is indoctrinated into prescribing antibiotics, vaccines and drugs, for every symptom a patient presents them with. Most of the time, symptoms are blamed on the patents mental health. Those physicians who speak out and offer alternative methods of healing that work, are censored and suppressed. Such is the sad state of affairs we find ourselves in today.

CHAPTER 13

Critiquing The China Study

I could not help but to mention The China study in this book. It is often referenced and referred to by vegans and plant-based pundits, as if it is some type of nutritional bible, which has solved all of mankind's diseases and nutritional conundrums. In my opinion, the book lacks some fundamental reasoning and logic. The book is authored by T. Collin Campbell MD, and asserts that a multi-decades long study done on rural populations in China, found data points which correlate the consumption of animal protein and fat with cancer and other diseases.

Food blogger and researcher Denise Minger, had published an article with a most outstanding critique. She examined Campbell's data points and found that his interpretation of the data points were mostly flawed. The original data source is published in a book called, *Diet, lifestyle and mortality in China.* It is filled with 800 pages of data and information. Campbell's interpretation of the data was completely absurd and biased.

Campbell had spent a large portion of his career experimenting on lab rats. In one of his studies, he experimented with concentrated and isolated forms of animal protein called casein. Casein is a protein found in milk. Casein, when isolated and concentrated, is incredibly difficult to digest and absorb. It is a very common food allergen in low quality milk, let alone in contracted and isolated forms.

Campbell fed the lab rats various levels of casein in addition to poisoning them with afloxtoxin, and observed how they reacted in terms of cancer growth. The rats suffered from legions and scarring in the liver, followed by tumor growth. He found that he could turn tumor growth on and off by removing or reintroducing casein in the diets. When rats were fed more than 5% of their diet as casein, they would suffer from faster tumor growth and die sooner. Campbell went on and decided to extrapolate the harmful side effects of refined, highly concentrated, and isolated casein protein, onto all animal protein.

There is no logic in his conclusion. First he decided to damage the livers of the rats by exposing them to aflatoxin, which is a known cancer causing carcinogen. This alone distorts the study. Next, he fed them concentrated and isolated forms of a milk protein which is notorious for it's indigestibility. It is not comparable to meat proteins or even high quality, whole-food milk ferments and yogurts. His conclusion that animal protein is cancerous and plant protein being safe is unfounded.

When he repeated the studies using isolated and concentrated forms of wheat gluten, which is a plant protein, the tumor growths were the same. It was not a matter of food input, but highly concentrated and isolated, difficult to digest proteins, in conjunction with aflotoxin, that caused the cancer tumors to grow.

A second flaw in his findings, were linking animal protein consumption to diseases where there were no links and correlations. He measured total cholesterol and used it as an intermediary variable between animal products and disease. He looks at various diseases in the original data for the China Study, associates them with high cholesterol levels and in turn animal food consumption. He used cholesterol as a marker for animal food consumption, but the intake of sugar may also raise cholesterol. There is no single association between consumption of animal products and diseases, but he resorts to intermediate variables in order to justify his conclusions.

The most glaring flaw in his argument was that he had a preconceived goal at proving animal foods cause disease. His pursuits and research may not have been objective. Campbell decided to omit data which correlated wheat consumption with heart disease. The data points in the China Study actually have links associating high consumption of wheat with heart disease. His quest to validate his hypothesis and preconceived notions associating animal foods with disease, handicapped him from the ability to examine and analyze the data objectively.

CHAPTER 14

The Politicization of Veganism & The Great Reset

As of late, there has been a constant barrage of vegan and plant-based propaganda from international institutions, media outlets, celebrities and athletes. Although there is some merit to removing packaged and processed foods in favor of a whole-foods, plant-based diet, the idea that simply removing all animal foods will lead to greater health and wellness is simply unfounded. There is no consideration of the developmental properties which are exclusively found in only animal foods. Much of the vegan public relations campaign that has become so popular as of late, are driven by powerful organizations such as The World Health Organization.

The outlets used to pedal the public relations campaign span from The New York Times, The Atlantic Magazine, Harvard College of Cardiology, and even outlets such as Netflix, which has been flooded with pro-vegan documentaries in recent years. Organizations such as The British Medical Journal associated eating meat with smoking cigarettes. Many of these documentaries and media outlets are merely the mouthpieces of international organizations and corporations who have their own agenda. They aren't reporting the truth, science and facts, but merely regurgitating propaganda.

One of the bedrock studies which the vegan propaganda rests on is a World Health Organization study in 2015, which linked consuming meat with colon cancer. The news of their findings spread around the world and percolated into media outlets, spurred documentaries, and even into public health and nutritional policy. The World Health Organization (WHO) was supposed to publish the full expose of their findings and research which amounted to 800 papers in total. To date, they have never shared the scientific rational or foundation of their findings. They never even shared the data to be peer reviewed by other journalist and scientist.

The studies of the WHO were based on epidemiology which is a very weak and sub-par science that can only show association but not causation. You can find correlations between anything using epidemiology, such as associating number of hours spent playing video games with divorces, or amount of hours one spends driving with cancer. Epidemiology relies on self reported data which is notoriously unreliable.

In the field of nutrition, epidemiology relies on food frequency questionnaires, asking how much of what food was consumed in the past months or years. When this type of research is tested and the questionnaires are examined against the actual food consumed by the participants, it is found to be largely inconsistent. Most people do not remember what they ate the prior day, let alone the past year.

The International Agency for Research on Cancer (IARC) was the branch of the World Health Organization which carried out the research. They looked at cross-sectional studies and uncontrolled longitudinal studies, instead of using the gold standard of studies, controlled longitudinal studies and randomized controlled studies. Additionally, the IARC panel only looked at 23 papers and not the 800 papers as initially claimed. Further, the majority of the IARC panel had spent over the last two decades publishing papers against red meat. Majority of the staff and panel leaders were vegetarians as well. They did not disclose this, as it is a conflict of interest and introduces an element of bias into the research.

The supposed mechanisms for which they blamed on red meat causing cancer were heme iron and N-nitroso compounds found in meat. David Klurfeld was a member of the IARC panel who has been very vocal about his frustration and issues in working with the group, and the nutritional dogma it was steeped in. According to him, the conclusion on heme iron causing cancer were based on studies where rats were fed blood sausage. Blood sausage is 80% blood and hardly any meat at all, this makes it abnormally high in heme iron. Further, the damaging effects of excess heme iron were only observed in calcium deficients rats but went away when the rats were fed calcium. Calcium directly competes with the absorption of iron in the GI tract.

David Klurfeld also protested against the argument for N-nitroso compounds causing cancer. He stated that the N-nitroso compounds that were being fed to the rats were being fed at levels that are a multitude of what humans actually consume, in even meat heavy diets. His concerns about the exaggeration of the data were ignored by other panelist and panel leaders.

When large, mega grain, seed-oil, and sugar producers, first wanted to wean out meat in favor of their toxic plant foods in the middle of the 20th century, they demonized meat's saturated fat and cholesterol content. Through controlling and sponsoring the education at major universities, public relations campaigns, and propaganda, they convinced the public that animal fats were culprits for heart disease.

In modern times, as the lipid-heart hypothesis has fallen out of favor with the advent of high fat diets and the age of information, the corporate-oligarchy and the vegan zealots have come up with new scare tactics. The agenda to drive out meat from the diet is an ideological and financial driven campaign, which is not actually steeped in science, or considerate of human health.

The reasons for this ideologically driven campaign to root out meat from the diet are multifaceted and there are multiple different groups who work in concert for a common aim. One of the reasons, and perhaps the most powerful reason it is being peddled, is because of the planets problem with overpopulation, resource drain, and climate degradation. There simply is not enough resources to continue feeding the mouths we have with the current political, social and economic models.

Since the industrial revolution, we have consumed the planets resources for commercial and industrial purposes without any consideration for the ecology. Although as I will explain in a later chapter, I believe if we shift to a more eco-conscious and regenerative paradigm, we could with great comfort sustain a population ten times the size we have now.

Due to ecological die off and mass extinction which climate scientist are now presenting to world leaders and influential members of the global corporate-oligarchy, there has been a unanimous decision to change the current paradigm. This paradigm shift is referred to as, "The Great Reset" by The World Economic Forum. The World Economic Forum is an independent international organization which brings together the foremost political, business, cultural and other leaders of society, to shape global, regional and industrial agendas.

The initial introduction of grain fed, cage operated, factory farmed meat, provided a protein and caloric boom to the world, which saw population growth sky rocket over the last century. Although it is unethical, damaging to the environment, inhumane, and of low quality nutrition, factory farmed animals nonetheless provided food for rapidly growing nations.

That era is now over and can not be tolerated anymore. The environmental consequences of not only factory farmed and cage operated meat, but also petrochemical agriculture, which is the production method for most of our plant foods, have been amongst the primary contributors to the planets ecological die off and climate degradation. Although I agree with the need to change the system, I do not agree that the problem is solely a consequence of meat consumption livestock farming. The problem is multifaceted, the way the mega corporations raise livestock for food, as well as their production of plant foods, deplete soils, poison the land, poison the air, poison the waterways, and poison the very food we eat.

In addition to reducing the impact on the planets resources and ecology, the removal of meat from the diets of the "herd", would lead to higher rates of infertility. Because saturated fat and cholesterol are precursors to all sex and steroid hormones, a diet without animal products would inevitably lead to a less fertile populace. Already today, with the prevalence of the USDA food pyramid and The Standard American Diet, which is practically vegan and plant-based, we have seen an epidemic of infertility. Fertility clinics have popped up in droves across the nation and young couples are having extreme difficulties in conceiving children. The level of infertility which we are witnessing in the 21st century has had no historical precedent. It is not only improper diets low in animal fat, but also environmental toxicity which is contributing to the infertility endemic.

The public relations campaign regarding veganism has nothing to do with human health as much as it has to do with the planets health, and the culling of the human population. Those at the top of the current political hierarchy are eugenicist, who view the majority of people as mere consumers, who are to be restricted from offering their contributions to the genetic pool of mankind's next generations. At current, there are "meat taxes" which are rapidly gaining popularity in the developed western democracies, including Australia. In places such as New York, the intention of these meat taxes and introduction of fake-meat alternatives, is to slowly wean out all animal products from the diet of the consuming masses.

In places such as New York, trends such as Meatless Monday have been introduced into the meal programs of public schools. Instead of removing the candies, processed foods, snacks and chips, refined sugars and seed-oils, it is the meats that are demonized and removed. Plant-based eating clinics have been introduced to multiple boroughs within New York City. Patients can meet with dietitians, doctors, and health coaches, who will guide them towards plant-based diets. What is starting now as a minor trend, is meant to engulf public schools, hospitals, cafeteria's, and fast food restaurants, over the coming decades. Removing meat will only result in an even larger intake of seed-oils, refined sugars, toxic grains, and indigestible vegetables.

The Meatless-Monday movement in New York City is funded by beyond burger, a fake-meat, alternative burger, for hungry vegetarians. Instead of trusting their instinct which hungers for meat, they opt in favor of soy-burgers, because they have been brainwashed to believe it is a healthier alternative. Large propaganda posters are displayed in public schools with absurd statements such as, "livestock production creates more greenhouse gas than the entire transportation sector". The removal of meat foods is an ethical offense, as these kids need the nutrients in meat more than anyone else during their developmental years.

In 2019, The EAT LANCET Commission out of Sweden published global dietary recommendations, with a focus on planetary health and sustainability. Their report garnered attention by governments world wide. The dietary recommendations advocate for high amounts of seed-oils, high amounts of refined sugar, lots of plant fibers and no more than 1/2 ounce of red meat, which is about the size of a gum-ball. The Physicians Committee for responsible medicine have publicly advocated for a meat tax to be introduced.

Another interesting fact is the number of unwanted births which the "elite" also want to curb with dietary manipulation. In The United States alone, there were 629,898 abortions in 2019.[15] Countless more children were conceived of by accident into families or single mothers who did not have the social and economic securities, nor the psycho-spiritual prerequisites needed to raise and develop healthy children. Delinquent children often result from such couplings who go on to reproduce more psychologically traumatized delinquents.

Powerful members of society who are responsible for helping to shape and guide human culture, view the replacement of animal fats in the diet with soy burgers, as a means to further curb fertility rates in underprivileged communities. Members of underprivileged communities are not usually concerned with health, and the replacement of fast-food meat patties with soy patties that tastes identical, would render no difference to them.

It is due to these ecological concerns and reasons that the vegan zealots and animal activists have received so much more support, attention, and most importantly, organized funding in recent years. Where as vegans were once on the fringes of society, and were notorious for being weak, anemic, ill, grey, pasty and frail, today they have

---

[15] Kortsmit K, Mandel MG, Reeves JA, et al. Abortion Surveillance — United States, 2019. MMWR Surveill Summ 2021

become a mainstream culture with popular celebrities and films endorsing such diets and lifestyles. There are countless vegetarian doctors who publish a plethora of books advocating for different types of vegan diets who are very well-funded. There are also very popular youtube personalities who are animal activist, masquerading their cult under the guise of science and nutrition.

The combined efforts of international organizations and large corporations, have usurped American politics in regards to nutrition and health. Dietary guidelines from The USDA which are shaped by these forces, have very influential and far reaching power. What the corporate-oligarchs decide in regards to the publics dietary and nutritional needs, percolates into USDA feeding programs, all health associated professions, including the American Medical Association, American Diabetes Association, American Academy of Pediatrics, and The American Nutritionist and Dietitians Association. From these organizations, the ill-founded dietary and nutritional guidelines make there way into hospitals across the country, where dietitians, doctors, nurses and nutritionist merely follow orders and parrot what comes down from the top.

Physicians, nutritionist, nurses and dietitians who work for large medical practices, and offer any advice that is contrary to official guidelines, risk medical malpractice and their licenses revoked. **Of course, there are thousands of physicians, nurses, doctors and nutritionist, who have stepped out of line and spoken out.** Without these individuals, my own work and understanding would not be possible. Several of these heroic individuals have been quoted and referenced in this book.

The new paradigm of conscious physicians are advocating for the food pyramid to be turned upside down. It is obvious to them that their patients who come into their offices suffer from disease and illness, despite following The

USDA food guidelines. Guidelines which advocate for 5 to11 servings of inflammatory grains a day, in addition to rancid seed-oils, and very limited, truly nutritious, animal foods.

The problem with turning the food pyramid upside down, is the economic blow black that would result in such a paradigm shift. The pharmaceutical industry would lose their most profitable income streams, medical doctors could no longer function as salesmen for the pharmaceutical industry, researchers would risk losing funding from large corporations, and big food companies would lose revenue, due to the shift in dietary patterns, which would favor foods from small family farms.

These conscious physicians, nurses, nutritionist and scientist, who advocate for the paradigm shift, are often often attacked, labeled quacks, isolated, and often have their lives destroyed. Instead of debating the science, the establishment and their parrots attack the character of those who think differently or offer new ideas. The most common form of undermining those who do not fall in line with official views is to claim that they are funded by the meat, milk or dairy industry.

Examples of well respected professionals who have had their careers attacked are individuals such as Professor Tim Noakes, who is a highly respected sports medicine professor. He merely tweeted that it was safe for mothers to wean children onto a low carbohydrate diet, which resulted in a three year long court process defending his medical license.

The politicization of veganism is a large concerted effort, by large corporations, cultural shapers, international organizations, and governments, who use the animal activist and the vegan cult zealots as mere pawns to push forward their agenda. I must conclude here, that I don't necessarily disagree with aims of their goals, which is to curb ecological and climate degradation, but I believe it could be done in a more harmonious manner, that would be more beneficial for all parties involved.

CHAPTER 15

Dietary Solutions Amongst a Sea of Nutritional Dogma

I will here address the dietary conundrum. I am sure I have confused many readers who thought that by partaking in vegan and plant-based diets, or by conforming with USDA guidelines, that they would at least be following the healthiest diets possible. The fact of the matter is, that the healthiest diet possible is a high quality, omnivorous diet, with which you feel the best. **Ideally, you would want to follow a dietary pattern that is similar to your closest cultural ancestors.** It best to follow eating patterns similar to your ethnic and cultural background.

The bodies take time and generations to adapt to new, whole-food diets and lifestyles, in order to sustain optimal health. It can not be done in one generation. There are some cultures who consumed very high amounts of animal fat such as the Inuit, or Maasai. There are others who were on the opposite end of the spectrum and consumed large amount of carbohydrates such as the natives of New Guinea or The Okinawans of Okinawa, Japan. The carbohydrates they consumed were not toxic grains or cellulose, but starchy roots and tubers from extremely healthy and mineralized soils. These people sustained superb health despite being on carbohydrate diets, however, they coveted the animal fats in their diet as well and placed the utmost significance to them. The Okinawans who have about 60% of their calories coming from carbohydrate have a religious attachment to their pork.

Some individuals advise high carb or high fat diets because of a certain isolated tribe or people who's dietary patterns reflect macronutrient intake that they advise. This is silly. The Inuit who were very robust and strong people consumed walrus, sea lion and whale fat, however, most modern people who even attempted to bite into such fatty pieces of meat would perhaps break their jaws, as well as face extreme difficulty and nausea with trying to digest such rich sources of fat. The best fat sources for us are the ones which are most readily recognizable by our bodies. For some, it may be walrus meat, for others it may be lamb fat, and still others, it could be fat from camels, sheeps and cows. The key is to find food sources that are ancestral consistent.

Another very important consideration is the intended goal of any person who partakes in any diet. My recommendation for macro-nutrient intake and dietary recommendations would vary depending on the intended goal of an individual I am advising. There are diets which are more suitable for growing babies and developing children, another for teenagers, another for young adults, another diet for those who want to boost their immune system, another for hormonal health, and another for longevity. They would all have many commonalities but macro-nutrient intake would vary. The advice of a well-seasoned nutritionist who is not subject to the dietary dogmas of the establishment could help immensely in this regard. Older people interested in longevity and anti-aging would do far better with less carbs. Conversely, children and developing young adults, would fare better with ample amounts of properly prepared carbohydrates added to the diet to aid in growth and development.

To reiterate again, individuals who come from ancestral cultures who consumed higher amounts of healthy carbohydrates in conjunction with nutrient-dense animal foods, would do much better sourcing foods which replicate their ancestral diets. A high carbohydrate diet in addition to nutrient-dense animal foods may suite them well.

The key here is the inclusion of nutrient-dense animal foods in proper proportion, the reduction of fruit sugars which were never available in such quantity and year round, the elimination of non-organic and improperly prepared grains, the elimination of industrial seed-oils, the removal of all packaged and processed foods, and finally the inclusion of organic plants which are ancestrally consistent. To properly digest plant foods, it is imperative to ferment plant foods.

It is important that I reiterate here that plant fiber cannot be digested by the human digestive tract. Human cultures also did not consume raw cellulose such as the raw salads advocated by narrow-faced and anemic vegan nutritionist today. Traditional cultures fermented raw plants in order to make them more digestible.

The removal of improperly prepared and non-organic grains alone would mean the elimination of pastas, bread, crackers, bagels, chips, cookies and cereals. Most often these foods are improperly prepared grains sourced from commercial farms. Properly prepared grains are artisan breads such as sourdough, which are intelligently fermented in order to reduce inflammation and increase bio-availability, as well as digestibility. The grain-based food of commerce produced by the large food corporations are trash food which harm the body.

White rice and potatoes are extremely nourishing and safe carbohydrates as well. They were both consumed across Eurasia and in The America's for many centuries. White rice is a carbohydrate staple across Asia. Now that you have a novice understanding of plant biochemistry and their defense mechanisms, you should understand why white rice is consumed by so many cultures. White rice is simply black of brown rice, which has had the bran and husk removed, in order to eliminate the plant defense mechanisms which would otherwise damage our guts.

The idea of what makes a healthy diet was solved a very long time ago by mankind's ancestors. They simply understood their environment and ate directly from it. They understood how to properly prepare the plant foods and to hunt the game and fish which the land offered. By obeying natural law, they were healthy and fit. Mental illness and physical illness were unknown in the isolated and harmonious cultures of our ancestry. The food and health dilemma was solved long ago. There is nothing new under the sun. The problem is with our current cultural paradigm which is totally unprecedented. We do not obey natural law and seek financial profits at the expense of other peoples health.

We have an overabundance of food which is grown from nutritionally depleted soils. Grains which are improperly prepared and grown. Rancid seed-oils, which are produced industrially and added to everything. High amounts of refined sugar, which are also added to most foods. And finally, the most silly, the removal and deprivation of dietary animal fats. The inclusion of animal fats, in proper proportions that the body can handle, is the single largest contributor to the rehabilitation of ones health. No isolated vitamin, mineral or supplement, could replace the need for animal fat in the diet. The foundation of this book is to convey this idea, that the public is being starved of the very food and nutrients they are most in need of, and it is only getting worse with dietary fads such as veganism.

CHAPTER 16

Livestock Farming as an Environmental Solution for a Dying Planet

The environmental concerns of our modern industrial farming practices should not be limited to only livestock production. Yes, cage operated, conventional livestock farming is a filthy, degenerative, unsanitary, inhumane, and unethical form of raising livestock. But if we are to address the livestock issue, then we should not ignore the agricultural issues which are correlates of equal measure. The entire paradigm of modern agriculture and food production is in need of an over-haul.

The current form of agriculture prevalent in The United States and all other industrialized nations, do not put into consideration the health of the soil, the food, the water, the air, or the rest of the ecological network of an environment. The petrochemical, mono-crop agriculture, which furnishes vegans with all of of their colorful, indigestible plant foods, are just as damaging to the environment as is commercial livestock.

In natural grass-lands, we find a diversity of plant, insect and animal species, that co-exist with one another to create healthy, interconnected, and interdependent living systems. Biodiverse grass-lands are destroyed and converted into dead zones for the sake of modern petrochemical agriculture. What were once diverse fields of wild grass-lands, are converted into mono-cultures, fields of wheat, soy, cotton seed, corn, green vegetables and other crops, destroying the ecology of the areas they are grown in.

These vibrant, ecologically diverse areas, which housed a plethora of different species, are converted to arid, infertile fields, for the purpose of growing a field of mono-crops with petrochemical additives. The native soil microbiology, the insects, and the animals, which once created the ecology of the field, are killed off due to the toxic effects of pesticides, fertilizers and herbicides sprayed on the fields. Our current agriculture is a direct contributor to the massive planetary die off and species extinction we are dealing with. The petrochemicals sprayed onto the fields kill off soil microorganisms, they pollute the soil for generations, they pollute the air, and wash off into water ways contaminating the global water supply, rivers and oceans.

Researchers on wild alligator species in Florida have found an alarming rate of decreasing populations and reductions in penis sizes. The male alligators were found to have abnormal levels of low testosterone and the female alligators were found to have low levels of estrogen, both markers of infertility. The culprit was found to be DDT and other agricultural pesticides, which found their way into water ways from commercial agriculture. Just as these agricultural chemicals are contributing to infertility and die off in wild species, so too are these petrochemicals contributing to infertility and diseases in human populations.[16] These agricultural chemicals are also significant contributors to the bee, monarch butterfly, and other other insect population die offs.

The amount of research which points at both, modern commercial livestock, as well as commercial

---

[16] Reduction in Penis Size and Plasma testosterone concentrations in juvenile alligators living in a contaminated environment. General and Comparative Endocrinology 101, 32-42 (1996) Article No. 0005. Louis J. Guillette Jr., Daniel B. Pickford, D. Andrew Crain, Andrew A. Rooney, and H. Franklin Perciva Dewed.

agriculture, destroying the planet, is overwhelming. It is not only these, but our very way of life, our consumption of resources which is not sustainable. 100 years ago, the average person had 20 to 40 pairs of clothe through the entirety of their adult life. Today, many people in industrialized nations go through that in a month! All of this drains resources from the environment and contributes to environmental degradation.

Popular documentaries produced by cult vegans such as *Cowspiracy,* have attempted to place blame only on animal livestock for the global water shortages. This is wrong and deceiving. Pastured livestock use rain water that falls on that land. The vegan climate activist use rainwater in their statistics when displaying the water consumption of livestock. Fresh water which has to be transported is consumed in far larger quantities by the grain fields and mono-crops of modern commercial agriculture.

70% of the worlds fresh water reserves go to irrigating crops. The non-rain water that is consumed by commercial livestock is consumed in the form of the grains they consume. Cows are not meant to consume grains, this breeds diseases and consumes far more resources then would otherwise be spent, than if livestock were raised on pastures. On a natural, regenerative farm, livestock use rain water that falls on the land and graze on what the land offers. Grain is added occasionally only as a supplement. In commercial live stock operations, cattle and livestock are not living on pastures, but on desert lots that breed disease.

The solution which I would offer, is for those vegan and environmental activists to take a proactive charge in combatting the issues which they are so passionate about. Instead of working to take food away from people, they should work to farm on permaculture principles, and provide better food, better air, better water, healthier soil, and healthy ecology to the people and planet. There are alternative farming practices which regenerate the ecology in contrast to commercial farms which destroy it.

These farming practices are often referred to as permaculture, regenerative agriculture, and holistic land management. It is a way of farming and raising livestock, which prioritizes the health of the planet and people first and foremost. It takes into consideration the ecology of the land, the microorganisms in the soil, the insects, the animals, the nutrient content of food, the health of people, and even the ecology of wild areas in proximity to the farm. It prioritizes all of this before corporate profits. If we are to avoid a climate and ecological catastrophe, it is inevitable that as a global society, we transition to this form of agriculture.

When one learns of the farming principles and techniques of these practices, they could gain a more profound respect and appreciation for animals, not only in the diet, but also in the management and care taking of the planet's ecology. Animals play an integral role in the planet's ecology which have no substitute. It is the healthy, biologically active manure of animals, in free range farms, which fertilize and feed the soil.

Individuals who are interested in these ideas can look into the works of iconic regenerative farmers such as Joel Salatin, amongst many others. Joel Salatin has spearheaded regenerative farming ideas such as **holistic cell-grazing**, which mimic the migratory patterns of herd animals in nature. The idea is that it was migratory animals, their manure and trampling of that manure into the lands, which created the rich, fertile soil, which we have now depleted over the preceding generations of petrochemical, agricultural practices.

Holistic Cell-Grazing

The herbivorous animals have a very specific role in nature which contribute to healthy ecology. Their grazing of grasslands, trim grasses and forage, which is converted into their animal protein and fat. They up-cycle the nutrients from vegetation into their flesh. Herbivores then pass biologically active excrement in their urine and manure, which feeds the soil with nitrogen, healthy bacteria, minerals and vitamins. This directly contributes to healthy, ecologically diverse lands and ecosystems. It is the manure of animals which bring biological life to landscapes in natural systems and nothing else.

In wild nature, herds of grazing animals graze an area until they are chased off by a predator, or until their manure have sufficiently covered the grasslands, forcing them to move on to fresh pastures. The movement of the herd causes their hooves to trample the manure into the soil, where it reinvigorates the roots of the grasses and soil with biological life, minerals and untold number of life giving qualities.

The grasses grow back stronger and healthier after their pruning and fertilization by the herds of herbivorous animals. This is how biomass is generated in nature. The grasses come back stronger, longer, and create an environment that is more favorable to more diverse species of grasses, insects and animals. These diverse grasslands with their abundant bio-mass sequester carbon from the atmosphere and produce fresh oxygen, reducing global CO2 levels. In addition to sequestering carbon, they provide ecosystems and habitats to a wide array of species ranging from microbiological life forms, to insects, bugs, reptiles, foxes, coyotes and so on.

Farmers who practice holistic land management, replicate this pattern but enhance it to an even greater extent. The method they use is called **holistic cell-grazing**. Farmers divide up their land into multiple cells which are cordoned off by electric wire. Once cordoned off, herbivorous animals are allowed into a single cell. They are allowed to graze on and trim the grass only up to a certain point, where they are then moved to the next cell.

This form of grazing allows farmers to preserve the roots of the grass by preventing overgrazing, which could cause desertification. In the time that the cell receives it rest period, the animals move from one cell to the next. During the rest period, each cell incorporates the fertilizing and life giving qualities of the manure which were received during the grazing period. This period of rest gives a chance for the cell to generate new biomass, and more diverse flora and fauna. The result is that, with larger grasses and more biomass, you have created a landscape which is more efficient in sequestering carbon from the atmosphere, and at the same time, providing more clean oxygen. It is a most genius practice based on the very principles of nature.

The conventional form of livestock farming does not respect the herbivores role in nature. Commercial livestock are concentrated onto feed lots, into a single cell, and fed grains which are not their natural food. The concentration of the animals onto feedlots, concentrates their manure onto a single plot of land, contributing to disease and environmental degradation. The roots of any grasses which may have been on the land before are consumed, causing desertification. The land does not get a break to regenerate itself.

Their manure is instead concentrated in large pools, which often find their way into and contaminate waterways and rivers. It has no contribution to the soil, the air or the environment, but instead degrades it. It does not contribute to biomass development in anyway. The animals are not allowed to freely graze on pastures, nor are they herded in an intelligent manner, but instead locked up into a single cell, with dirt floors that are more akin to a concentration camp.

A study funded by The National Institute of Food and Agriculture examined farms and soil health in The American State of Georgia. The soils which were examined were from the farms of farmers who transitioned from growing row-crops, to producing milk from grass-fed cows. The farms were converted to green pastures.

"We found that converting cropland to rotational grazing systems can increase soil organic matter and improve soil quality at rates much faster than previously thought possible in a system that sustains food production," said the study's lead author, Megan Machmuller, who worked on the three-year project as a doctoral student in UGA's Odum School of Ecology. She is now a postdoctoral fellow at Colorado State University.[17]

In my own experiences working on a multitude of different farms and on land regeneration projects spanning three continents, I have also found that nothing helped to regenerate land, produce biomass, and develop food forest systems, as quickly as integrating animals into a cell grazing system. I have experience with numerous methods of land care such as inoculation of soils with microorganisms using compost teas and rock-dust, as well as the introduction of nitrogen fixing species of plants in conjunction with swales.

All of these efforts, which although do work, require far more labor and time than letting the animals do the work. The results of so called "veganic" farming, are futile and laughable when compared to the results achieved with livestock cell-grazing in terms of biomass production and

---

[17] Farmland management changes can boost carbon sequestration rates. J. Merritt Melancon. May 11, 2019.

soil microbiology amalgamation. Every true farmer and environmentalist who has any experience with the different methods, knows that this is not an issue up for debate. Man can not do better than mimicking natures systems.

Another pioneer in the field of environmental activism and reversal of desertification is Zimbabwean scientist Allan Savory. An iconic ecologist, he states that only livestock and the mimicking of migratory patterns in nature, can heal the planet and reverse desertification. He believes that by creating healthy grasslands through holistic cell grazing, we can sequester atmospheric carbon, deoxygenate the atmosphere, and regenerate ecology. His statements are not based on his feelings but on real world experience.

He initially believed that grazing animals and herbivores were responsible for the climate degradation due to overgrazing of land, resulting in desertification. This is still the popular consensus amongst many environmentalist and so called "eco-conscious" vegans. Allan Savory, as well as other scientist, had advised governments in Southern Africa to slaughter or cull 40,000 elephants from the wild in order to stop desertification. The operation failed to reverse desertification and degradation of landscapes, despite killing 40,000 elephants.

Allan Savory called his decision to advocate for the slaughter of large numbers of wild elephants in Souther Africa as "the saddest and greatest blunder of my life". The prevailing world view at that time was that too many grazing animals were contributing to desertification of landscapes, similar to what is proposed in the popular vegan documentary, *Cowspiracy*.

Soon after his initial blunder, Allan Savory continued with determination to find solutions to climate, land, and ecological degradation. It was during his travels to America where he saw that National Parks were also in rapid decline and desertification, despite not having any livestock graze the grounds for over 70 years. He continued to examine research plots all over the Western Half of The United States which had cattle removed, and found that it had not stopped the desertification process. American scientist and researchers had no answer for why the desertification process continued unabated despite the removal of cattle.

Allan Savory realized that mature grasses which are not trimmed or subject to biological decay by herbivores before the next growing season, end up further degrading the landscape and soil. If grass's fail to be consumed and trimmed by herbivores, then they end up oxidizing in the dry season, which kills the grasslands and the soil. The oxidative process shifts the grassland from a green, lush landscape, into one that is woody and dry. This creates barren soil and releases carbon into the atmosphere. Restricting cattle and herbivores from the landscape and the ecology does not help with desertification and climate change.

Today, Allan Savory insists that the only option is to use livestock and mimic the migratory patterns of herd animals in an intelligent design, in order to reverse desertification and regenerate landscapes. His results using herbivorous animals to regenerate land projects in Southern Africa and around the world are outstanding and inspiring. He has regenerated entire landscapes which were desolate, dry and barren, into thriving grasslands with river systems coming back to life. Prince Charles called him, "a remarkable man". Iconic regenerative farmer Joel Salatin wrote, "History will vindicate Allan Savory as one of the greatest ecologist of all time". He has a very popular lecture available on youtube where he presents his work in a TEDx lecture, *How to green the world's deserts and reverse climate change, Allan Savory -Youtube.*

"We have now in the violent horn of Africa, pastoralist planning their grazing to mimc nature and openly saying it is the only hope of saving their family and saving their culture. 95% of that land can only feed people from animals. I remind you that Im talking about most of the world's land here that controls our fate, including the most violent region of the world, where only animals can feed people from about 95% of the land. What we are doing globally is causing climate change as much as I believe fossil fuels and maybe more. But worse then that, it is causing hunger, poverty, violence, social breakdown and war, and as I am talking to you, millions of men, women and children are suffering and dying. And if this continues, we are unlikely to be able to stop the climate changing even after we have eliminated the use of fossil fuels. I believe I've shown you how we can work with nature at very low costs to reverse all this. We are already doing so on abut 15 million hectares on 5 continents. And people who understand carbon far more than I do, calculate that for illustrative purposes, that if we do what I am showing here, we can take enough carbon out of the atmosphere and safely store it in the grasslands soils for thousands of years. And if we just do that on about half the worlds grasslands, we can take us back to preindustrial levels while feeding people. I can think of almost nothing that offers more hope for our planet, for your children and their children and all of humanity."-Allan Savory

CHAPTER 17

The Ethical Debate

As for as the ethical debate is concerned, I do agree with vegans that the nature of cage operated and factory farms is inhumane. However, I do not agree that animal livestock should be shunned completely. Instead, the commercial livestock model should be transitioned to the regenerative farm model, which rotate the animals in a cell-grazing system, and work harmoniously with the land and animals. This is entirely possible to achieve with every single animal farm in the industrialized world, but simply needs attention, effort and willingness to change.

As far as the actual consumption of the meat itself, I would argue that it is not my choice wether I consume meat or not. We humans are obligatory carnivores. Without meat consumption, we simply fail to thrive. Our physiology is designed for and requires meat consumption. There are ways of slaughtering animals which are humane and have been practiced by high cultures and traditions all around the world. One example is the Halal method practiced by Muslims, whereby they cover the eyes of the animal, ensure that the animal is in a tranquil state, and then proceed with cutting the jugular vein, in order to insure a fast, painless death.

Many would still argue even against these points, and state that we should consider the feelings and lives of animals before our health. Or even worse, they masquerade their cult under the guise of health, and claim it is not needed for optimal health. The truth, the science, and the facts, regarding this cult diet which I have belabored on in this book, as well as the personal experiences of tens of thousands of ex-vegans, are not in agreement with such claims.

I consider my own health, the health of my family, and all other human beings, before I would ever consider the life of an animal. My priority and activism is towards the well-being of the entire ecosphere, humans included. Many vegans seem to have no empathy for humans. I would argue that they don't actually have empathy for animals either. A brain and body which is starved of cholesterol, cannot afford to feel empathy.

Many who have been indoctrinated into the cult and subject to it's dietary torment, simply do not have the brain malleability to change their perspectives. The brains are starving of nourishment and cannot create new synapses, new connections for learning and memory. How can such a starving person feel empathy? I propose that veganism is merely a form of narcissism which allows vegans to feel a sort of deluded superiority complex.

I propose that the most ethical way of eating is to obey nature. There is a natural cycle in the food chain which requires our consumption of animal foods. The bacteria in the soil play their role and consume the minerals in the form of hard rocks. Plants fulfill the next role in the uptake of these minerals into their structure. Next, come herbivores and than the carnivores. We humans, are at the top of the food-chain, and because of this, it is our duty to be caretakers of the natural world. We are not to disobey natural law, but to enhance natures patterns and embrace her rules. When we die, we will also return to the soil, feeding microorganisms and plant life. The ecology on earth is a closed loop system. To eat what we are designed to eat, to obey natural law, is to be spiritual.

CONCLUSION

My hope is that this book was of significant aid and assistance to all those who are objectively seeking truth in regards to nutrition. We are overwhelmed today with a constant barrage of vegan propaganda, which makes difficult the task of discriminating between what is true and what is not.

If one desires to lose weight and detoxify, it makes sense to perhaps undergo a vegetable and fruit-juice fast, provided one has ample amounts of fat-stores. Aside from weight-loss, it makes absolutely no sense to destroy oneself on a vegan diet. It is not healthy, it does not help the ecology or planet, it is not sustainable, it has absolutely no merit. The only case where it would make sense long term is if individuals were sincerely opposed to consuming any animal foods at the expense of their health. There is no arguing against that, each may do as they wish.

I am sure, that the majority of people who become vegan do so with noble intentions. Though the current generation of Western Civilization's youth are perhaps the most well-intentioned people to ever walk the face of the earth, they are unfortunately misguided by opportunism and lack in wisdom. It is my belief, that the hope of the planets ecological future rest in the hands of these people. Never before have such a people manifest who are more interested in the health of the ecosphere than they are of their own financial prospects.

I understand that the idea to just go vegan and save the planet may have seemed attractive and easy, but the fact of the matter is, that these dietary trends and ideas are merely ploys by the corporate-oligarchy. To truly create change, for the welfare of the whole planet, not just the animals, but the insets, the air, the rivers, oceans and even humans, we must put our hands in the soil and return to the land. The world needs regenerative farmers.

We can also vote and make changes with our dollars, supporting not the mega-food corporations, but small farms which contribute to ecological regeneration. The matter of animal and ecological welfare requires of us much more active participation than merely slapping a hipster dietary label upon ourselves. At this current time of massive planetary die off, the planet's ecology needs authentic human beings who are not subject to the degenerative cultural influences of Hollywood and the corporatocracy, but are rather, sovereigns unto themselves. Individuals who understand their connection with the natural world, and are willing to arm themselves with the shovel. To become natural human beings again is the call from nature.

Due to our current way of life, the entire ecosystem is in peril. Narcissistic vegans who can only contribute pictures of themselves with their colorful foods are of absolutely no use to us. What we need is individuals who are willing to take a combative approach to climate change with the mobilization of urban farms. The entire food system needs to be over-hauled. It must become local, organic, regenerative, and include animals as well as plants.

As I write this book in the winter of 2021, there are massive, global and geopolitical changes underway, which are designed to pull the rug out from underneath our narcissistic and consumeristic civilization. There are very powerful players in the global chessboard who have decided that a controlled, self demolition of the world economy, is the best way to rapidly transition us into a new paradigm and avert climate catastrophe. This new paradigm, often referred to as "The Great Reset" by The World Economic Forum, is intended to place the needs of the natural world before the excessive greed which is naturally ingrained into capitalistic societies.

Individuals who find their sense of self or identity in their countless numbers of designer merchandise, will no doubt have a hard time coping with the changes which are unfolding. For those in whom the human spirit is still alive, we have an opportunity to participate in this transition. It entails a harmonious relationship with the natural world, which benefits our health as well as the health of the planet's. It requires of us a return to soil, to land, to the natural world. It requires of us to return to that original, noble role, which was endowed upon humans by nature, to become caretakers and stewards of the natural world.

Additional Titles By This Author

NUTRITIONAL FORTIFICATION AND PHYSICAL DEVELOPMENT
AUTHOR VARIS AHMAD

Nutrition & Hair Loss
A New Perspective On Male Pattern Baldness, Telogen Effluvium, Alopecia Areata
BY VARIS AHMAD

THE DISEASE OF KINGS
THE RAW FOOD NUTRITIONAL BASIS FOR THE RISE & FALL OF CIVILIZATIONS

Living Foods & Bioenergetic Nutrition
Vitality • Consciousness • Raw Vegan
Varis Ahmad

For personal consultations, The Author can be reached at
polymathva@gmail.com

The author can also be found at

https://www.youtube.com/c/VarisAhmad

Made in the USA
Monee, IL
03 January 2023